# Anti-Bias Curriculum for the

# Preschool Classroom

# Anti-Bias Curriculum for the Preschool Classroom

by YWCA Minneapolis Early Childhood Education Department

Redleaf Press®
www.redleafpress.org
800-423-8309

Published by Redleaf Press
10 Yorkton Court
St. Paul, MN 55117
www.redleafpress.org

First edition 2021
Senior editor: Melissa York
Lead contributing writer: Paula Landis, MA, curriculum director, early childhood education
Cover design by Jim Handrigan
Interior design by Becky Daum
Typeset in Minion Pro
Printed in the United States of America
28 27 26 25 24 23 22 21        1 2 3 4 5 6 7 8

Cataloging-in-Publication Data is on file with the Library of Congress.

Printed on acid-free paper

# Table of Contents

PREFACE     vii

CHAPTER ONE

**Our Story**     1

CHAPTER TWO

**Anti-Bias Teaching**     9

CHAPTER THREE

**Self-Reflective Practice**     31

CHAPTER FOUR

**Families: The World of Children**     46

CHAPTER FIVE

**Domains and Standards**     60

CHAPTER SIX

**Anti-Bias Observation and Assessment**     118

CHAPTER SEVEN

**The Anti-Bias Classroom: Lesson Planning, Teaching, and the Learning Environment**     133

REFERENCES     161

INDEX     167

# Preface

Two key international experiences have dramatically affected our YWCA Minneapolis community during the process of writing this book: the COVID-19 pandemic and the killing of George Floyd. The COVID-19 stay-at-home orders, layoffs, and deaths laid bare already existing health and financial disparities, and broad public awareness continues to grow. As the pandemic continued through the summer of 2020, conversations in early childhood education centered on business solvency for the field at large, driven by mounting worries about educating children as centers closed and families struggled to work while caring for their children, either as essential workers or from home, and many others lost their jobs entirely.

Then on Memorial Day 2020, police killed George Floyd in one of our communities in Minneapolis, Minnesota. The pain from this death is enormous. It has, among many things, brought forth highly essential and emotionally charged conversations and actions for many people on personal, workplace, educational, and governmental levels. All along, there have been myriad voices besides ours in our communities calling for massive changes in policies and practices in nearly every sector we can see. But now these calls are being heard in the context of these larger societal events, lending these issues greater urgency in the public eye. We want to take this time to state some of our present thoughts on the way this book might resonate during these times and in the times to come.

To us, to be anti-bias means looking for a multitude of ways to create equity for all diverse people. As you will see in our second chapter, the intersections of race and ethnicity, sex and gender, culture, religion, and economics, to name a just few, are infinite. We do not expect this book to be a complete history or conversation about how each of these areas of human diversity affects people. In fact, the ways in which human diversity affects people are individual, and to some extent individuals are done a disservice when we make generalizations regarding human diversity. Social change is a complex issue, and we are glad that now is a time when the importance of change is heightened. It is important to realize that anti-bias work is a constant, conscious decision. This book is not meant to be used as a standalone resource for understanding the complexities of social climates but rather as a resource and a reflection of some of our work at the YWCA Minneapolis.

We recognize that our mission to eliminate racism and support women is essential for the health of our future. We know that our skills and awareness move and change over time. Like a single observation of a child, this book is a small snapshot of what we have learned and built in our anti-bias early childhood education practice. We hope that our openness is an invitation to learn more and build stronger communities dedicated to justice for all the people we reach as a result of this publication. We believe in the power of self-reflection as a tool for anti-racism and anti-bias work for children and ourselves. We hope that this book spurs impactful ideas for your work in the early childhood field. Thank you for reading our book.


Warm regards,

The YWCA Minneapolis Early Childhood Education Department

# CHAPTER ONE
# Our Story

## *How did we get here?*

YWCA USA is one of the oldest and largest multicultural organizations in the world. Our mission is to eliminate racism, empower women and girls, and promote peace, justice, freedom, and dignity for all. YWCA Minneapolis is a trusted social justice organization with a more than 125-year history of advocacy for women and children. We serve more than 30,000 people in our community every year through award-winning programs, classes, and workshops.

As part of the national YWCA USA and in coalition with thousands of community members, public and private businesses, and policymaking bodies, we strive every day to achieve the following:

- race, ethnicity, and gender equity
- economic independence for women
- respect for diverse cultures
- a place where children and youth thrive
- a vibrant and healthy community

YWCA Minneapolis carries out this work through five departments:

1. Health and Wellness
2. Girls and Youth
3. Racial Justice and Public Policy
4. Early Childhood Education
5. Organizational Advancement

From the beginning, YWCA Minneapolis has been at the forefront of the mission to advance diversity and inclusion. This book is part of a powerful legacy. We humbly offer this knowledge, earned through years of mission-based advocacy within our community. For more information about our history, please visit us online at www.ywcampls.org.

## Our History: An Organization Shaped by Suffrage and Civil Rights

### 1859

The YWCA USA starts in Boston, Massachusetts, in 1859.

### 1891

The YWCA Minneapolis is founded as a member of YWCA USA, with Mrs. W. A. Miller as board president.

YWCA Minneapolis is one of the first and few women-owned and -operated buildings in Minnesota. It calls for equal pay for women, runs women factory worker retreats, and defies sexist social norms by opening an indoor, year-round pool for women.

### 1927

Seven years after the Nineteenth Amendment to the US Constitution is ratified in 1920 to include women's right to vote, the YWCA Minneapolis runs a fundraising campaign titled "What's a Girl Worth in Minneapolis?" It was the first capitol fund drive, and it raised more than a million dollars for the new YWCA building.

### 1940

In the 1940s, under board president Phebe Mae Givens, the YWCA Minneapolis helps find homes for Japanese Americans who had been imprisoned in internment camps.

### 1945

YWCA Minneapolis is the first Twin Cities organization to offer a racially integrated swimming pool.

## 1963

In 1963, Dorothy Height, YWCA USA leader and president of the National Council of Negro Women, was instrumental in organizing the March on Washington. She is often called "the godmother of the civil rights movement."

## 1970

In the 1970s, the YWCA Minneapolis starts pregnancy prevention programming and provides early childhood care and education. We also begin offering seminars aimed at combating racism.

## 2000

In 2000, YWCA Minneapolis opens the largest YWCA health and fitness center in the country. The Midtown YWCA houses our third YWCA Minneapolis early childhood education center.

## 2007

In 2007, YWCA Minneapolis Channel Challenge swimmers cross the English Channel to raise awareness about racial disparities in drowning deaths in the Twin Cities. Swimmers raised money for youth swimming programs. Children in our centers continue to receive free swimming lessons today.

## 2010

In 2010, the National Association for the Education of Young Children recognizes the YWCA Minneapolis Downtown Early Childhood Education Center as an Engaging Diverse Families exemplary program. Our center was one of only ten programs nationwide to receive this honor.

## 2013

In 2013, our Early Childhood Education Department is one of the largest nationally accredited nonprofit childcare and education programs in Minnesota.

## 2019

In 2019, the YWCA Minneapolis Racial Justice department leads its 17th annual It's Time to Talk: Forums on Race. This event brings more than 1,200 diverse leaders from business, education, arts, and community service agencies. They came together to move Minnesota forward through honest conversations about race and ethnicity.

YWCA Minneapolis remains committed to empowering women and girls and eliminating racism. Our leaders, employees, members, and partners hold themselves to the highest standard by continuing to listen, learn, grow, and act. This work is lifelong and transformative. Success depends on communication, responsiveness, and a wholehearted dedication to uncovering and combating bias in society and in our own practice.

The YWCA Minneapolis Early Childhood Education (ECE) Department partners with families to build a vibrant and healthy community. As one of the largest nonprofit providers of nationally accredited childcare in Minnesota, we serve a wide range of community members, including families who are new to the country. Our efforts toward equity forged our anti-bias curriculum. Since 1976, when the first children's center opened in downtown Minneapolis, we have seen our system work. Consistently, more than 90 percent of children enrolled in the YWCA Early Childhood Education Program meet school readiness indicators, irrespective of their socioeconomic status, race, ethnicity, or national origin. We think our teachers are doing something very special. We believe these results come from strong dedication among our teachers.

In 2010, Minnesota called on early childhood education programs to use approved curricula tied to a common rating system. This system would allow parents seeking care for their children to compare the quality levels of participating programs. Ratings indicated the level of quality care and educational structure that parents might expect. The new system also had an impact on program finances. Centers that proved their quality could expect greater support. For more information on this rating system, please see Parent Aware at www.parentaware.org.

YWCA Minneapolis was excited to participate in this rating system because it showcases teacher and center quality and gives parents more power to choose a program to meet their needs. We explored the approved curricula. In an effort to find the right fit for our centers, we asked the following questions:

- Does this curriculum guide educators to celebrate the individual culture and learning style of each student?
- Can lessons be shaped and reshaped by the lives of our students and families?
- Does it provide tools to listen and respond to the social needs of the community?
- Does it reinforce our mission: to eliminate racism and empower women and girls?
- Would it inspire a growth mindset for teachers that allowed them to lead their own development?
- Is play-based learning a key principle in this curriculum's philosophy?
- Does this curriculum confront bias and encourage safe learning spaces for children from communities who often are failed by our educational system?

We found that while most of the current published curricula granted some flexibility for teachers to meet the needs of individual children and encouraged play, they were not proactively anti-bias. We think being explicitly anti-bias is a key driver of success. We wanted anti-bias practice and play-based learning to be front and center in our defined work.

We also believed our teachers should be able to express themselves. They should continue to build on the excellent work that has taken us so far. The learning that happened in their classrooms made a difference. Our success rate proved it! Our ECE department had demonstrated that the proverbial "kindergarten readiness gap" will not persist when the privilege of high-quality early childhood experiences is accessible. For more than ten years, our teachers have been focused on equity, education, and play-based learning. We think this is no small victory. We decided to formalize and share this framework so that all children have the opportunity to learn in equitable environments.

It was not easy. Until we decided to formalize our process, the YWCA Minneapolis anti-bias curriculum was crafted through the lived work of teachers. We relied on a patchwork of trainings, the mission, and the voices of parents and students to guide our practice. The next step was to connect our work to science-based early learning standards.

We conducted field research. We observed our teachers in action to determine how they demonstrated excellence in each of the learning domains. We recorded anecdotes that illustrated anti-bias caregiving and play-based learning. We documented the skills teachers used to support kindergarten readiness for all children. The data we gathered laid the groundwork for this book. It gave us the opportunity to share our practice with you.

Parent Aware, the accrediting body of ECE programs in Minnesota, approved the YWCA Minneapolis anti-bias curriculum framework in 2014. That same year, our board of directors encouraged us to share our learning with the early childhood education community at large.

The YWCA Minneapolis anti-bias curriculum is guided by the following principles:

- Self-reflection is essential.
- Families are partners.
- The center environment must reflect home culture.
- Children learn through play.
- Teachers must take children's and parents' thoughts, ideas, and feelings seriously.
- Teaching is individualized: differences in ability and learning are celebrated and respected.
- Teacher advocacy can eliminate oppressive educational practices and create safe, vibrant learning space.

Our curriculum focuses on the caring ways relationships are formed between children and teachers. This book offers a guide to both the art and science of teaching in an early childhood setting. Even better, it allows you to approach your work from an anti-bias perspective. You will have the tools to embrace the diversity in your community. You will be better equipped to ensure that all of your students thrive. It will not be easy. You will not be perfect. We are not perfect. We never will be. True anti-bias work requires a willingness to learn and grow . . . and learn and grow . . . and learn and grow.

## Bringing It Together: A Flexible Framework

The structure of the YWCA Minneapolis preschool anti-bias curriculum is a flexible, living framework. It is aligned with state and national standards. Here are its objectives:

- We follow each child's lead and explore the learning domains through play.
- Our play uses materials from the child's world and home life.
- Teachers weave anti-bias practice into all aspects of learning.
- Teachers document what happens in play and shape their lesson plans based on these observations.
- Teachers change their practice based on continual observation and assessment of children's growth and development.

Flexibility requires sensitivity. Effective teachers adapt and change when necessary. For example, when children engage deeply with an activity, we allow extra time for sustained play. Flexibility does not mean we abandon all structure, ignore standards, and embrace chaos. We can view learning standards as a destination for the children and curriculum as the way teachers and children reach that destination. And, of course, the scenery is fascinating! Children learn best when all aspects of learning are connected to concepts they are interested in. The most engaging early childhood curriculum incorporates learning opportunities—the ones that include real-life activities and pretend play—into every part of the day.

## How to Use This Book

Each chapter of the YWCA Minneapolis anti-bias curriculum explores and explains our guiding principles. Each chapter builds upon the one before it, but you can read them in any order that suits your needs.

In chapter 2: Anti-Bias Teaching, we discuss our current understanding of key questions we keep in mind when we deliver high-quality early childhood educational experiences. The first question, "What is bias?" includes defining discrimination, prejudice, and microaggressions. Next we discuss modes of unfair bias, such as racism, homophobia, sexism, classism, and religious and political bias as opportunities to construct equity and fairness. We next share our perspective on the specific needs children might have in terms of physical, emotional, and cognitive development and ways teachers can support differences in their settings. Last, we share our goals for anti-bias work and how they can each be supported in simple interactions with children.

In chapter 3, we focus on self-reflection. Our willingness to learn about ourselves helps us recognize the perspectives of others. We share our investigation of this process, and what we have found are some of the ways self-knowledge can invigorate and elevate our practice.

In chapter 4, we focus on families. Since each child views the world from the vantage point of home culture, we believe that the best curriculum is the one that connects with not just the whole child but also the whole family—and often the whole community as well.

In chapter 5, we connect anti-bias work with high-quality learning standards. We describe how anti-bias teachers can set goals in the following learning domains:

- Social and Emotional Development
- Approaches to Learning
- Language and Literacy
- Creativity and the Arts
- Mathematical Development
- Scientific Thinking
- Physical and Motor Development

In chapter 6, we offer tools for teachers to measure and support children's success through observation and assessment. We share how our process encourages active play-based teacher-child interactions as the best place to collect observation and assessment data. We believe children are partners in this process, and when they are included, it can actually lighten the load teachers carry.

In chapter 7, we provide an overview of lesson planning. This guide will help teachers integrate our key pillars of quality—anti-bias and play as the vehicle toward learning goals—into the daily classroom environment.

Some curriculum books lay out specific activities and units, but you will soon see that we refrain from this approach. Instead we contextualize ways to support children's play and developmental goals within an anti-bias practice and build readers' understanding of how to do this in their own classrooms. Children reach the teachers' developmental goals through play. We focus on giving children time to engage and play with concepts and materials. Through play we are teaching for understanding, rather than teaching for knowledge or skill alone. We think that to do this requires the following:

- Teachers cultivate an intentional anti-bias teaching practice.
- Teachers understand child development.
- Teachers set learning goals and plan accordingly.
- Teachers use conversations and coaching during play activities to help children understand and transfer concepts.

This book provides strategies and stories to show you what implementation looks like in our programs. We also offer questions to help you analyze your classroom interactions, relationships, and outcomes. Our goal is to promote teaching that is grounded in anti-bias principles. Consequently, we must continuously evaluate our own life experiences and teaching practices.

Because anti-bias work asks us to confront both internal and external prejudices, answering these questions may make some readers uncomfortable. Some of the scenarios our teachers shared were uncomfortable experiences. Some of the topics we discuss and scenarios included may be triggering for some people who have experienced discrimination in their own lives. We honor where everyone is in their own journey, and encourage everyone to recognize the moments that they feel discomfort throughout this process. It is not easy to confront bias, racism, sexism, homophobia, and ableism. Admitting our own bias is not easy either. Are you a person who has experienced injustice? Are you a person who has unwittingly added to a biased interaction? How is your experience different from someone else's? Everyone's experience will be different, each are equally valid, and everyone has anti-bias work that can be done.

We are grateful that our teachers allowed us to publish their stories about self-study, communication, and empathetic understanding. We changed the names and markedly defining details of teachers, children, and families' stories. We did this to both protect privacy and to show how common many of their experiences are.

In this curriculum, we think of you, the reader, as a lifelong learner. Effective leaders in early childhood education share a passion for professional development. In her book *Leadership in Early Childhood* (2012), Jillian Rodd describes three main characteristics of early childhood leaders. They are

- curiosity in learning;
- courage to take risks, make mistakes, and learn from them; and
- compassion for one another, to develop trust and create high expectations among colleagues.

We hope this curriculum will give you the opportunity to be curious, take risks, and cultivate compassion. We hope to inspire you to be anti-bias advocates. Then you can inspire your colleagues, your colleagues can inspire theirs, and so on. We think this is an attainable and essential goal to have for our communities, our children, and ourselves. We think this commitment is one essential component needed for building a strong foundation in anti-bias preschool education. A program without a commitment to anti-bias work can be harmful to children and its stakeholders. We are all in this together, and together we hope to continue to build communities committed to equity through anti-bias work.

# CHAPTER TWO
# Anti-Bias Teaching

## *What is anti-bias teaching?*

People often wonder "What is anti-bias teaching?" or, "How can you be anti-bias?" This chapter outlines some concepts and terms that help us explain our understanding of anti-bias teaching. It also introduces some of the professional development tools YWCA Minneapolis (YWCA) teachers use to shape their anti-bias teaching practices.

Generally speaking, bias is harmful when unfair consideration is given to one group over another. Yet personal bias is present in every aspect of an individual's awareness. The American Psychological Association (2006) reminds us that bias very often precedes prejudice. When we speak about bias, often the first words that come to mind for someone are racism and sexism. These are often the easiest concepts to access, but they are not the only ways in which bias can lead to prejudice. In this book, we have focused on racism and sexism as the two primary forms of bias used in examples because of the moment in time that we are in. The #BlackLivesMatter movement cresting in a new crescendo, and the continuing work of the YWCA to combat sexism, has meant that those areas are the ones in which we have the most experience and the most examples. In a little over 200 pages, we regrettably do not have time to fully address all of the possible areas of bias and where they might intersect, but hope to touch on many throughout this book. As a backdrop to everything we are discussing here, we encourage you to reflect upon the compounding impact of injustices due to intersectionality.

We also want to recognize that for people who have more than one historically represented and persecuted identity, the intersectionality of those identities only compounds the biased experiences they may have; it also may impact the bias an individual may feel. The APA strongly warns us all to take notice because bias can hurt us all now and has hurt many of us in the past. We take this to mean that unchecked bias can lead to negative prejudice and unfair discrimination. We have found *Anti-Bias Education for Young Children and Ourselves* by Louise Derman-Sparks and Julie Olsen Edwards (2010) to be an excellent resource to help understand and stop unfair bias. You can also see the American Psychological Association (APA), the Anti-Defamation League, and the glossary in this book for useful definitions and steps to take to help address bias. Our practice is confirmed in what the APA and others have also researched and reported. Bias against groups of people can be based on many factors, including race, ethnicity, gender, familial status, education, physical appearance, ability, economic status, sexual orientation, culture, or religion. Jacob Priest and colleagues (2020) recently contributed to our collective understanding of how bias hurts people. Their study finds that discrimination is a socially sustained and inescapable stressor for African Americans that impacts health. It is not possible to accurately consider health and wellness of African Americans and

other historically marginalized people without deep consideration of the ways racism and other forms of prejudice are woven into every aspect of life. Unfair bias can affect the way expressions, thoughts, and even objects are viewed. Nina Asher (2003) reminds us that it is critically important to remember that the concepts of diversity and unraveling bias are extremely complex. Like Asher, we know we are all connected. And like so many researchers in the field, we believe it is vital that we confront and eliminate unfair bias in our perceptions and in our educational system if we want to build healthy and vibrant communities.

It is important, required, and possible to teach and learn about prejudice, discrimination, and unfairness with young children (Beneke, Park, and Taitingfong 2019). They also explained that early childhood educators are often untrained in ways to teach about fairness, which may cause them to avoid discussing sensitive topics like race. We think that it is our responsibility to teach and build equity through an anti-bias approach. Sometimes people think their child is too young to benefit from an anti-bias curriculum, because they may not yet be aware of any differences among their peers. But children notice differences at an early age, especially in social contexts like a preschool classroom (Park 2011).

We have seen that too, and we teach them to! Younger students learn to name colors and shapes.

Older students learn to group and categorize similar objects.

Children notice differences in people's physical appearances and in how they do things whether we consciously address them or not. In our classrooms, we often hear phrases like:

"Her hair looks different than mine."

"I don't eat that at home."

"I don't understand what he's saying."

"Why is she wearing that?"

"Why is he being pushed in a chair?"

These types of questions and comments can lead to meaningful learning experiences, because anti-bias teachers are always on the lookout for opportunities to explore and honor differences. One of our teachers, Ms. Chantal, affirms her group's perceptive observations by proclaiming, "Everybody's different!" Whenever she says this, her class echoes it back.

Another teacher, Ms. Dana, shared that one of her students always asks, "Is that Spanish?" when he hears another language. Ms. Dana sees this as an opportunity to talk with her students about the many languages of the world.

Caryn Park (2011) suggests that preschool children are noticing racial and ethnic differences and making meaning about what they see with the information they have in social contexts. Her analysis suggested that children will help each other make sense of things, like race and ethnicity, that are beyond their current comprehension, especially when there is no older or more experienced person available to help. Children leading children in understanding racial and ethnic differences can lead to incorrect ideas, she said, and it is the role of the teacher to critically and carefully guide children's understanding about human differences. We agree that people are not born with prejudices, but as they grow, children quickly learn about stereotypes from the adults and media around them. As teachers of young children, the language we use and the comments we make can dramatically influence children's perceptions of human differences. It is important to use an anti-bias framework to speak accurately, calmly, and with respect when talking about differences.

YWCA teacher Mr. Jaxson used this approach with one of his students, Tyler.

One day after school, Tyler walked up to a mother picking up her child. "Why are you fat?" he asked.

Mr. Jaxson stepped in. "Tyler, every person's body is different and special," he said. "When we talk to others, we use facts. I think you might mean her body looks different from your mother's body. Is that right?"

Tyler nodded.

"Okay," Mr. Jaxson said. "Let's try saying, 'I think your body is different from my mother's.'"

Tyler repeated Mr. Jaxson's words. His eye flicked between the mother and his teacher. Mr. Jaxson smiled, made eye contact with them both and nodded his head.

Mr. Jaxson's short but important conversation with Tyler helped show him the significance of choosing his words carefully. His actions showed the others that this was a supported learning moment. Mr. Jaxson gave Tyler a high five for "using fact words."

Often it is the adults in the room who are uncomfortable talking about differences, but professional development can help us approach these discussions with confidence. Beneke, Park, and Taitingfong (2019) understand how Mr. Jaxson might be feeling. They said teachers sometimes freeze when a sensitive topic is broached by children. And, when they do address it, they must somehow rise above possible feelings of sadness, guilt, shame, or a host of others to present a calm, educative, and supportive demeanor. That is hard work! Knowing that we are learning alongside children and families to address and unravel unfair bias can be protective for teachers as well as children and families. Acknowledging that we are all learners in stopping unfair bias can help teachers feel less overwhelmed or unduly burdened in their endeavors. It is an unending process, after all.

In addition to acknowledging the teacher as a learner in stopping the spread of unfair bias, teachers also have a unique call to understand the developmental stages of children. Understanding children's developmental capabilities will enable them to teach through an anti-bias approach. A skilled teacher can guide conversations in ways that are meaningful and appropriate. It is important that we do not shy away from these situations, because research shows that anti-bias learning does not happen on its own.

Here is an example from our own work that supports Park's (2011) findings that without an adult to guide them, a child may easily come to untrue or unfair conclusions. When one YWCA teacher heard a child being described as a baby by her peers, she quickly stepped in and explained that they were preschoolers. When the students asked why the other child could not use the bathroom and do other self-help tasks by himself, the teacher told them that everyone learns different things at different speeds. The children agreed that everyone needs extra help once in a while, and the teacher led them in a conversation about the things they still needed help doing. They wrapped it up by celebrating the things everyone, including their classmate, could do well. Because of this teacher's quick thinking, the children's conversation was steered in a much more positive direction.

When we model and encourage open dialogue, we help children become more comfortable with each other and more confident about exploring new ideas, customs, and ways of being. Respecting diversity is an essential component of anti-bias teaching. When teachers take the time to address with mindfulness and care any issues that arise, we can help create the educational and professional climate we want.

## Celebrating the "Whole Child"

The word is out—all human beings are unique. And when children walk into a classroom, it is as if they bring their parents and families too—and their ways of knowing and understanding life.

Urie Bronfenbrenner and Stephen Ceci (1994) explain this through a model of human ecology. The human ecology model views children's development as affected by all the different systems they are a part of—such as family, school, or learning environments, places of worship, and neighborhoods—and examines how those systems interact with one another. Within the human ecology model, there is also the individual response; that is, two children from the exact same circumstances will still express themselves in their own ways.

Anti-bias practitioners are driven to take a closer look at their students in order to truly see, celebrate, and serve the whole child. When we do, we cannot help but become advocates. When we care about the total individuality of our students, we are motivated to combat racism, sexism, and other forms of oppression. We are also motivated to give our students the skills they need to advocate for themselves.

We believe that best practice is achieved only through teaching from an anti-bias perspective. We know the conversation about anti-bias started in early childhood programs long ago and continues today. We think many experts would agree: there is no effective conversation about best teaching practices—in any field—that does not emphasize the need to confront bias.

## What Is Bias?

Bias happens when we value one group—their ideas, opinions, expressions, and lives—above another. Bias is reinforced by stereotypes, and both stereotypes and bias lead to prejudice and discrimination. Microaggressions often occur in environments that fail to confront and combat bias. We broadly define these terms so we can organize our understanding of the negative consequences of bias.

Bias is not inherently negative. Although bias is not limited to gender, sexuality, religion, race, ethnicity, ability, or economic position, we look at these general categories to develop an awareness of how we can support and celebrate, rather than ignore or devalue, the differences around us. From a culturally responsive perspective, Susan Bennett and colleagues (2018) draw on a rich body of research to explain that ECE centers are formative of culture—and even as they shape culture, they are shaped by it. To us this means that the ways in which culture is present or not present in children's daily classroom lives affects both self-image and learning.

Ibram X. Kendi (2019) in his book *How to Be an Antiracist* covers many important aspects about his path to understanding racism and bias. One point he made is that to undo unfairness we have to favor a marginalized group over a privileged one. This might be startling to some. Today, for example, it is more common to see representations of women astronauts or doctors. Once, that was pushing social boundaries. Now, you might find centers with photos of gay or adoptive families. A person who feels threatened by such images may say something like "I feel marginalized when there are not photos of [heterosexual couples, Christian-themed holiday décor, and so forth] in the environment." To that, we say it can be painful to feel some loss of ground, but remember that our culture privileges white, heterosexual Christians already, so there is no need to overshadow others with dominant imagery. In our settings it is okay to bring unexpected messages to the preschool classroom.

Things we ask ourselves are these: How are marginalized groups represented in the classroom? How are women and people of color physically represented? For example,

| TERMS | DEFINITION |
|---|---|
| **Stereotype** | Unfair, exaggerated beliefs or distorted truths about a person or group. Allows for little or no individual differences or social variation. Based on images in mass media or reputations passed on by parents, peers, and other members of society. Can be positive or negative.<br>*Examples include the following:*<br><br>• *Women make better teachers than men.*<br><br>• *All little boys like to knock down block towers.*<br><br>• *All little girls like dolls and cooking.* |
| **Prejudice** | An opinion, prejudgment, or attitude about a group or its individual members. Is formed by a complex psychological process that begins with attachment to a close circle of acquaintances or an in-group such as a family. Often aimed at out-groups.<br>*Examples include the following:*<br><br>• *Stay-at-home parents are lazy.*<br><br>• *A person from [anywhere else] is less worthy than I am.* |
| **Discrimination** | Behavior that treats people unequally or unjustly based on differences.<br>*Examples include the following:*<br><br>• *Not allowing a child to play in certain areas based on gender.*<br><br>• *Allowing only English to be spoken.*<br><br>• *Anti-male diapering and toileting policies.* |
| **Microaggression** | A stereotypical, prejudicial, or discriminatory remark, often made without the speaker's awareness of its harmfulness<br>*Examples include the following:*<br><br>• *Asking a person of color or an Indigenous person where they are "really" from.*<br><br>• *Expecting a person from a marginalized cultural group to be a spokesperson for their whole culture.* |

can we see female doctors and astronauts of color in play materials? Do we have conversations that allow all people to share their perspectives without shame or blame? Do we show alternative ways of thinking without negatively privileging others? In a simple example, a girl says she wants the blue cup, and a boy says he wants the red. Does a teacher say, "That doesn't matter. You can each have whatever cup I give you." Or does the teacher say, "I hear you like red right now, is that right?" In this example, both answers sidestep the teacher's own reaction to the children wanting cups in colors that are not traditionally associated with their genders. If a teacher does have a reaction to that request, this is a moment to practice self-reflection about why it might have been triggering. The latter response statement might help the child feel seen, even in a way that seems small to an adult. Teachers must be aware of limiting how their own personal biases might impact their responses to the children.

It gets more complicated when the topics become more personal. What if a male child came to a teacher's room wearing a pink ruffled top and the teacher thought it was an inappropriate piece of clothing for the day? Does the teacher say, "I can't believe his mom let him wear that to school!" or "That shirt is too fancy and you are just going to ruin it. Here, put this on instead!" Or, does the teacher either not comment on the shirt at all, or choose to say to the child, "You have a pink shirt, and it has ruffles. What do you think of that?" Can you see the difference in passing judgment, no matter how small? In interactions with children, it is vital that all bias leading to judgment be stricken from the interaction. Sadly, intersections of other identities such as race, ability, and religion, often compound the trigger for a biased reaction. What if the child who wanted the red cup is a Black boy and the child who wanted the blue cup is a white girl? What if the Black boy is wearing the pink shirt? The myriad of possible intersections of identity in every situation is endless. Teachers must be poised to offer a compassionate response and cultivate an environment of respect for all children, families, and teachers. Teachers must be poised to offer a compassionate response and cultivate an environment of respect for all children, families, and teachers.

What if a center has not cultivated an open and honest dialogue with the people in their community, especially people from historically marginalized identities? How can centers work with their families to help foster conversations about cultural differences? How can a teacher not privilege the stereotypical white majority experience and viewpoint when the environment is a white majority? We believe educators must evaluate how mainstream beliefs and expectations influence what happens in their classrooms. It is not enough to say we respect diversity; we have to show it in our actions and materials. This is also not to say that one group is better than another. We want all people to feel seen and heard, because there is room for everyone at our tables.

We know unfair bias hurts everyone. And we know that teachers want their students and families to be safe, healthy, and successful. An anti-bias perspective helps us align our practice with this goal. We know there is a vast body of research that covers many facets of diversity and bias and many of the ways it can influence early childhood education settings. The research we have reviewed in this book is but a small sample of work that is available. Because the topic of diversity is so vast, the work mentioned here is only some of what has stood out to us recently. Next, we discuss areas in which we have seen unfair bias harm people. We focus on gender and race for the most part. Please be aware that this is not a complete volume on what bias can look like. It would be impossible to complete a book of that nature. In addition to gender and race, we mention several other topics, including disabilities, economic status, religion, ethnicity, sexual orientation, and others. Please be open to learning and growing with us as we tackle these difficult topics that affect us all.

## Negative Bias: Sex and Gender

It is common for the word *gender* to be connected to the long-standing practice of sexism. The YWCA Minneapolis was built to combat sexism. We think sexism is one of the longest-standing traditions of abuse in the world. From unequal pay to the current lack of women's equal rights under the US Constitution, sexism is a vibrant field of oppression that we walk through every day. Have you ever wondered why early childhood education is stereotyped as women's work? Katrien Van Laere and colleagues (2014) note that ECE has historically been work done by women. Most people's experiences would lead them to agree that women do make up the majority of the ECE workforce. The answer to *why* women make up the vast majority of the workforce and *how* it is related to sexism is complicated. A full discussion of this topic is beyond the scope of this book. However, one way to look at this is through an analysis of the ECE teacher workforce. Marcy White-book and colleagues (2018) in the *Early Childhood Workforce Index 2018* share data that shows women make up the majority of the ECE teacher workforce and are paid extremely low wages. They clearly assert that the wage disparity hurts women, who are also mostly mothers and women of color. In *The Early Care and Education Teaching Workforce at the Fulcrum,* Kagan, Tarrant, and Kauerz (2008) explained that low wages are an example of market value. They said that if the public valued caring for children and the women who gave this care, wages would reflect that regard. Following this line of thinking leads us to the question: "Does society value mothers, children, and particularly women of color less than white men and noncaregiver roles?" We talk more about racism in the following section, but it is also a reasonable question to ask here, under the topic of sexism against women. We think it is possible that a chronic devaluing of young children and women, especially low-income women of color, is at play.

This backdrop is one of the reasons the National Association for the Education of Young Children (NAEYC) Power to the Profession movement is focused on creating a well-compensated and diverse ECE teacher workforce. Sharon Lynn Kagan, Kristie Kauerz, and Kate Tarrant (2008) propose a plan for supporting the complex problems that the ECE workforce faces. Economic equity for women is just one part of its plan; we know money won't fix everything, and low wages in all sectors beyond ECE is an example of negative bias against women. On the bright side, the public perception of early childhood is changing. Today more than ever, people are realizing that investing in young children means a better future for us all. If you had asked us twenty or even ten years ago, we wouldn't have thought that people would commonly understand that some of our most powerful and impactful learning happens when we are under the age of five. Today it is common household knowledge that high-quality care pays off for all of us. We see a movement to increase the public respect for the teachers of young children.

Gender bias against women is not a problem to be solved in one sitting. It is a process that is ongoing. Given that the early childhood classroom is a place that both reflects and builds culture, it can be a location for building respect for women. For example, respect for women can be brought to the classroom through play materials. As you might expect, this work begins with individual self-reflection. Teachers can ask themselves what ideas they are bringing with them into the classroom. Then teachers and centers can provide materials that show women in sports and in construction roles, as police officers and as doctors, and in the military and in executive positions. These materials can help disrupt the pervasive, albeit slowly changing, landscape of what women can do and what importance they hold in society.

It is also important to support the work of caring and the value of nurturing. Do we encourage boys and girls both to care for the toys, dolls, or stuffed animals, for example? Do we support the open expression of feelings without stereotyping what girls and boys can or cannot do? We can have meaningful conversations about women and men in the workforce, valuing the work of teachers and supporting fairness in the classroom to set the stage for a more just society within our classrooms.

The expectation that only women are ECE teachers and the devaluing of their work through low wages is not the only aspect of sexism that comes into view when we talk about bias. We must also talk about the sexism against men and transgender and gender non-conforming people that shows up in the early childhood education profession. There is a large body of literature that is focused on men in early childhood teaching roles, yet after the first decade of the twenty-first century, men make up less than five percent of the ECE teacher workforce (Fenech, Sumsion, and Shepherd 2010). That statistic has remained largely unchanged. Several researchers strongly urge more men into the field because it will bring important gender diversity to it (Tokić 2018; Van Laere, Vandenbroeck, Roets, and Peeters 2014). The research is clear: ECE practice should seek to challenge dominant social patterns of sexism, which limit an individual's perception of available social roles. This tells us to hold gender diversity very dear in our classrooms, and we agree. At the YWCA, we actively practice the use of inclusive and personal pronouns, and in addition to urging more men into the field of ECE, we encourage transgender, gender non-conforming, and nonbinary people to join the field as well. (This said, we also want to recognize that it is not sufficient for any of these discussions to say, "If we just had more Black teachers, or male teachers, or women leaders," we would be free of our inherently biased structures. But, in practicing a commitment to self-reflection and anti-bias work, we will be ready to not repeat the pattern.

Jennifer Sumsion (2000) explains that there are complex reasons why men are underrepresented in the field, but having men in professionally caring roles would be good for all ECE stakeholders. Again, one way to encourage a greater diversity in the gender mix of teachers is to counter and reduce mainstream stereotypes. In our practice we assert that there is not one kind of man who wants to be an early childhood teacher, just as there is not one type of woman who can be a top business executive. The reality is that men are historically ostracized from the field of early childhood education just as women are guided toward it. Standing against sexism creates a climate where children see counternarratives to dominant social narratives. One of our male teachers has a sticker in his room that reads, "Men who change diapers change the world." The statement is a lighthearted contradiction to the very real and very damaging belief that it is "unnatural" for a man to be an early childhood teacher. Fears of men in the field range far and wide. Our perspective is that gender diversity is integral for showcasing the vitality in the role of teacher. We want children to know that caring for others is a sign of strength, no matter where we find it. We know most young children can't read yet, but a room with the message that a nurturing man is a benefit to the world is a powerful climate to bring them into. Think of the impact that hearing this message can bring. A child walks into the room with her mother and asks what the sign says. The mother says, "Men who change diapers change the world. That means men and women together care for little children, and that helps us all be healthy and happy." We value diversity at the YWCA; supporting the caregiving skills of all people is one of many ways we can do this.

YWCA teachers also use books, images, stories, conversations, and teachable moments to confront gender bias and sexism. We go into more detail about this in chapter 7, when we share the story of one teacher who turned a book loaded with gender stereotypes into a platform for critical thinking. Most important, though, is that teachers must rely on a rigorous self-reflective practice to challenge any personal bias that might affect our teaching.

The bias for or against a person because of gender can also be complicated by gender expression. For example, one teacher realized she felt uncomfortable with twin students who wore what she thought to be gender-nonconforming clothes. The male twin wore a fluffy pink sweater, and his sister loved her dinosaur shirt and navy-blue athletic shoes. When the teacher noticed her own personal discomfort, she sought the advice of her team. They helped her examine her beliefs, overcome her bias, and build a stronger relationship with the twins and their parents. This teacher realized her uncomfortable feelings about the children's clothing was coming from her own adherence to a stereotype. Stereotypes can lead us to prejudice. As another example, we have encountered some teachers who have homophobic beliefs. For example, we have heard that some teachers truly feel fear that boys playing with dolls will alter their gender expression. Gender expression is a complex issue, far too large for us to piece out in this book. But, the discussion of gender expression is a rich arena for creating equity. Gary Butler and colleagues (2018) explain there are ever-growing numbers of children openly questioning their gender expressions. They also suggest that even in preschool, children may begin experiencing a disconnection from their assigned gender. The researchers pleaded for a greater complexity of understanding gender, and we agree.

With regard to gender expression and sexual identity, we think children deserve a climate where they are free to explore and express themselves in a nurturing environment. Contrary to the belief of some, children who play with toys that are deemed culturally atypical for their gender will not somehow become sexually aligned with that gender. For example, not all girls who like trucks are lesbians, and not all boys who like to dress up and dance are gay, though sadly some teachers may hold this unfounded belief that what toys a child plays with can influence gender and sexuality. To this, there are two responses.

First, according to the Kinsey Scale, there is actually a seven-point measurement that can be used to determine a person's sexuality along the continuum from heterosexual to homosexual; this can also include an outside-the-chart measurement for asexuality. Gender identity and sexual orientation are not binaries (boy, girl; gay, bisexual, straight), but are fluid identifiers that can change throughout a person's life. And second in response to fears about child play influencing either of these identities, everything that is in the classroom is and should always be available for every child to play with from a developmental perspective.

An example of teacher self-perception can be found in Alexandra Arraiz Matute, Luna Da Silva, Karleen Pendleton Jiménez, and Amy Smith (2020). They discussed a pervasive stereotype that teachers are asexual. They asserted that many people in the LGBTQIA+ community do not feel safe to express their identity, even in an assumed liberal environment. They encouraged us to consider the double injury a member of the LGBTQIA+ community may experience in a homophobic social climate—first, that a teacher is presumed to exude a sense of asexuality, and second, that any sexuality present is assumed to be heterosexual and cisgender, so a person who is gay, transgender, or in any way uncomfortable embodying a socially dominate narrative of their own personal sexual and gender expression is further separated from a feeling of welcome in their environment. One preservice teacher in the study had felt that she was not welcome to share or show her identity as gay along with her teacher identity. This asexual act had been painful for her. Clearly a presumption of cisgender and heterosexuality identity can be damaging to some people.

Hidehiro Endo, Paul Chamness Reece-Miller, and Nicholas Santavicca (2010) contributed to this body of research a decade earlier. They said that queer teachers face hostility despite schools' push for diversity. They assert that gay is ignored, and classrooms are not considered a place for sexuality conversations, especially not in younger grades. A gay teacher can suffer under the constraints of two identities that are assumed to be at odds. If "gay" and "teacher" are not allowed in the same room either overtly or unconsciously, people might be tempted to adopt a "don't ask, don't tell" mindset. The study found standing actively against a "don't ask, don't tell" mindset can positively challenge gender stereotypes and bring greater awareness to the fact that gay, straight, or queer is not a person's only identity.

Both of these works resonate with us, and we take it to mean that teachers need space to be their authentic selves.

It is very difficult to hold all differences sacred or discuss all the ways people are diverse, even if they are close friends and colleagues. One teacher we know had cultivated a friendship with another teacher, a gay man. She explained in a professional development session that she had always "assumed that when he was talking about his partner, he was referring to a woman. I felt ashamed of myself for thinking this and confused. I never asked because I thought it was none of my business to ask for details. But when he corrected me in conversation, I realized I could have worked harder to get to know my friend." A proactive way we support space for teachers to be their authentic selves is through the practice of respecting people's pronoun preferences (she/her/hers, he/him/his, they/theirs, etc.). While pronouns do not always or only describe gender or sexuality, it is yet another way teachers can experience the social setting of teaching in an equitable manner.

Making space for teachers to safely be their authentic selves also sets the stage for children to have the space to explore how they want to express themselves in the world. In our classrooms boys and girls can wear what they like, dance, cuddle, sing, and create. We hope they grow into a world where people are safe to be who they are wherever they are. Some teachers and parents we have met have expressed worry about boys and girls experimenting with non-stereotypical gender activities. We approach this topic with a fluid response, because gender expression can be fluid as well. We believe people deserve the space to express their selves safely and without harm. We want to reiterate that we know the trifecta of sex, gender, and sexuality are extremely complex. We hope readers will explore more of these topics to bring a greater sense of equity into their personal and professional lives.

## Negative Bias: Racism

Like sexism, racism is another big issue the YWCA Minneapolis was built to address, and we have a mission to eliminate racism and support women and girls. Racism is one racial group's assumption and enactment of superiority over another racial group. The group in power receives direct benefits as a result. Racism is one of the oldest and ugliest ways people enact unfair power over others. Its roots extend deep into a shameful history of slavery and colonialism, and it is still very active today.

Racism, like sexism, is a complex and vast issue that often makes people uncomfortable. This could be one reason people resist discussing it. Knowing and acknowledging that racism is active in education today is part of an anti-bias teaching commitment. Many researchers, to different degrees, explain how knowledge about racism can be abstract (Derman-Sparks and Edwards 2010; Lin, Lake, and Rice 2008; Meece and O'Kelley Wingate 2009; and Ullucci and Battey 2011). When we think about racism as an abstract idea, we do not confront the racist thoughts and belief systems that are actively hurting our students and their families. Instead, we begin to blame the victim. In her book *Cultivating the Genius of Black Children*, Debra Ren-Etta Sullivan (2016) explains that one product of racism is seen when children of color are labeled trouble-some, less able to learn, or neglected by their families. In these types of scenarios, some teachers struggle to identify racism as the root cause of these beliefs.

How do we keep cultural bias from becoming racist labeling? Here, we describe the stages one of our teachers went through as she uncovered and confronted her own bias. This process moved her toward being a better parent partner and a more empathetic, well-rounded educator.

Ms. Alicia was frustrated. "Jessica loves playing in the sand," she told her director, "but her mother keeps insisting that I keep her out of the sandbox. Every day at pickup she is angry because she's dirty. I don't understand what she thinks. This is preschool. Children need to play and they get dirty! I've tried to explain the importance of outside play and the development Jessica gets from being in the sand."

"Why do you think she gets so upset?" her director asked. "There must be a reason."

Ms. Alicia admitted she did not know but guessed that Jessica's mother, Lisa, cared more about appearances than she did about Jessica learning.

Instead of relying on Ms. Alicia's assumptions, the director asked Alicia to set a meeting with Lisa to better understand her perspective and work to find a solution. The goal was to figure out if there was a way to allow Jessica to play in the sandbox while still meeting Lisa's needs at pickup.

During their meeting, Ms. Alicia said to Lisa, "I know picking up a dirty child is driving you nuts. What can I do to help?"

Lisa said she felt embarrassed when her child was messy in public, and if they had to stop somewhere on their way home, her embarrassment became even worse. Lisa also said she spent a lot of time doing Jessica's hair, and getting the sand out was nearly impossible: "The sand sticks to the oil, and it makes her cry when I clean it off."

Ms. Alicia realized she judged Lisa's response to messy play based on her own life experiences. That judgment was unfair. If it had continued, she might have labeled Lisa a neglectful parent who was not allowing Jessica to have the play experiences she needed to be a successful learner, although this was far from the truth.

Teachers often need to work hard to unravel their thoughts about situations like these. During reflection, Ms. Alicia said, "After talking with Lisa I realized that she has a very different perspective about a clean or dirty child. I realized I was assuming I knew what was best. I thought that letting a child get messy was a sign of 'good parenting.'"

Ms. Alicia's life experiences contributed to her bias. She was white and from a small Midwestern suburb. As a child, she loved playing in the sand for hours, and her family encouraged her to get messy when she played. Lisa was African American and from a large Midwestern city. She told Ms. Alicia later that her parents put a strong emphasis on staying clean, especially when at school. It was to the point that Lisa had two separate wardrobes: one for work and public life, and a completely different set that could be worn only at home.

This conversation with Lisa allowed Ms. Alicia to see things from a different perspective. Had they not sat down to discuss the situation, Ms. Alicia's bias may have negatively affected her relationship with Lisa and Jessica.

After their conversation, Jessica wore a hat while playing to help keep sand out of her hair, and Lisa brought an extra set of clothes for Jessica to change into before she left the center. Not only did teacher and parent work to support each other, but they were able to better communicate about the fun learning experiences Jessica had in the sand.

We know that not all people share the same ideas on any given subject, especially a sensitive subject like the cleanliness of young children. Because of this, we used this situation as a conversation starter for YWCA teachers in a setting where the teachers represented many different racial, ethnic, and cultural backgrounds.

After hearing the story of Ms. Alicia, Lisa, and Jessica, one teacher reflected that she had to be excessively clean and felt burdened by it as a child. She said she did not like having to be "shined up" by her mother and grandmother, and the oils and rubbing hurt her skin. She did think it was her family's response to a racist culture that created the feeling they needed to keep her looking clean so she would be accepted at school. Yet another teacher said she was taught by her grandmother to always look her best because her grandmother grew up with the experience that white people view people of color as dirty and ugly.

It is important to note that the skin in which Black people live in is a subject of contention that may start for many people from a very young age. As just one example, Jasmine Abrams and colleagues (2020) found that young girls were indoctrinated into gendered colorism, the racist ideology that light skin is preferable to dark skin. While there is a lack of research on the impact of this biased belief, and a lack of space in this specific book, we wanted to recognize that this exists as a form of bias and to honor the realities of the people who have experienced discrimination as a result.

In the same conversation another teacher reflected that he didn't remember a time where he felt public scrutiny for his appearance and that he didn't realize before that this difference could be linked to the privilege of being a white male; a Latina woman commented that she was "able to pass" for white and she didn't have to "worry."

This discussion went on to support further the teachers' reflections surrounding how students and their families might feel in public in their daily lives because of their skin color alone.

These perspectives show us that there is not one experience people have in response to racism. As an example, we can look at the work of author bell hooks. In her book *Teaching to Transgress*, hooks (2014) tells a story of how she felt joy in her all-Black elementary school and explains how she felt when forced to go to a newly integrated white school. She remembers how Black children were made to conform to white ideas, which meant they were never good enough as they were but were always having to succeed based on white standards. Not only did hooks experience and witness Blackness to be dishonored in her new school, but history shows that as a consequence of desegregation, Black teachers came to make up a smaller proportion of the profession, and Black children in integrated schools are taught by mostly white women in a persistent climate of racism. We think an act of anti-racism can be a call for more teachers of color and a diverse range of ethnicities.

We take this to mean that part of our work is to watch for strongly persistent attitudes against children of color today. Racism is not abstract—it is clear and present and not limited to racism toward only Black people. We ask ourselves, how might hooks's story connect to the teacher whose family taught her she needed to be aggressively cleaned or to the mother who was embarrassed of a "dirty" child? We wonder, in what ways do racist ideas imbedded in our society make people of color feel they are not welcome as they are but rather must seek to present a public image that is acceptable to a white majority? The teacher who remembered being "shined up" also explained that this aspect of her upbringing led to her having a very professional appearance, and she was proud of that. Racism is not a one- or even a two-sided coin. The process of understanding it is an ongoing life choice that presents new and more complicated realizations when we choose to seek them out.

Kendi (2019) reminds us to consider that unlearning racism is not a task only for one group of people because we are all affected by it. As a former schoolteacher herself, hooks would agree that being aware of bias can assist in unraveling racist labeling and make you a stronger educator. It takes a conscious effort to continue to strengthen your teaching. Below we discuss other cultural considerations in anti-bias teaching, including economics, religion, and politics. For additional reading on race and gender topics, we like Robin DiAngelo's (2018) *White Fragility: Why It's So Hard for White People to Talk about Racism* and Sara Ahmed's (2016) *Living a Feminist Life* in addition to the other cited resources.

## Other Cultural Considerations

We know that while there are general similarities or norms, each individual is a unique expression of their interpretation of their own cultural position. Teachers must work every day to be conscious of the biased messages they may send to and about families. Being insensitive to your own bias can be particularly difficult to perceive and correct. Because it would take volumes to address the vast variety of cultural differences that can abound in an early childhood education environment and it would still not be enough, we focus for only a moment on some broad topics for your consideration.

It is a common misconception that people of one cultural group share exact traits and beliefs. Andrew Gibbons (2011) reminded us that people who hold positions of power in schools are often part of the white Christian dominant narrative. Not examining this perspective can bring about a harmful assumed standard, since not even people who share the same church will view social experiences the same. In fact, Gibbons argues, the unique perspective and expression of each individual makes diversity an inescapable truth. This truth of diversity is why educators must recognize the dominant narratives in which they live and work, becoming more aware of the power dynamics inherent in educational standards and evaluations.

John Nimmo, Mona Abo-Zena, and Debbie LeeKeenan (2019) shared ways families' spiritual and religious experiences can be difficult for early childhood educators to navigate. But even in a white male Christian privileged culture, we can all work to build communities of inclusion that affirm all people's family cultural expressions of faith and spirituality without advocating for one over another. While it is inappropriate to show only Christian holiday images, it is also sterile to eliminate all aspects of faith and spirituality from a learning environment for young children. We agree with the researchers who advocate for "religious literacy," where children are taught to notice that religion is personal and cultural, and one is not more correct than another. We take this to mean that in anti-bias teaching it is important to understand that an individual's personal culture is nested in a larger cultural context. This means that all people have unique points of view that influence their thoughts, perspectives, and actions. We cannot take it for granted that one perspective is correct over another, and we must be on the lookout for ways individual culture influences all aspects of how we teach. One way to do this is to send overt messages to families that their practice of faith and spirituality is important in the classroom. By asking families to share artifacts, pictures, music, and other mementos

of their specific cultural practices, teachers can be encouraged to build relationships with their families, to find out what their families practice, and to invite families to come into class and share their heritage. While not all families may have the time, the interest, the availability, or the materials, doing this serves the dual-purpose of letting families know the classroom is an inclusive environment, while also reminding teachers that the dominant culture is not where holiday celebrations begin and end.

Communication styles are another aspect of personal culture that intersects with all areas of diversity. Communication styles are personal and cultural and can affect understanding or misunderstanding among people. As you work to develop your anti-bias lens, consider your verbal and nonverbal communication style. How are you interpreting the communication from the children and families with whom you are working? What tells you if a person cares about what you have to say? Why do you think this? When we investigate the lessons we were taught, we are able to see how our perspectives shape our teachings, our communication, and our ability to relate with center parents and other staff who may use a different approach.

To be more respectful to all our families, regardless of economic position or religious and political backgrounds, our teachers made the following changes:

- Teachers stopped using food in art projects when they realized these activities were troubling for families that faced food insecurity or for families who viewed food as a blessing and not a toy.
- Since families use different forms of currency, we made an effort to think through the payment options we use in songs and activities. For example, when we invent lyrics to "The Wheels on the Bus," we ask the child, "Who is with you on the bus?" so we can include parents, other caregivers, or significant people who slide bus cards or pay bus fares with change.
- We avoid praising clothing based on how new it looks. Some families do not have the disposable income to buy new things. We call attention to the color, texture, individual style, or functionality instead.
- Religious celebrations and teachings are supported when they are authentically connected to students and people in the center. We check with families to learn how to best support them and connect with them during holidays.
- The YWCA is careful to take a bipartisan political stance, but we believe an ECE center has a great impact on the kinds of citizens our students will become. We are responsible for transforming the world in which they will grow up. This means teachers from all backgrounds and affiliations work together as advocates for social justice.

At the YWCA, we consciously work to avoid assumptions about people based on their cultural affiliations. We serve individuals and understand that everyone experiences and expresses their beliefs in unique ways.

## SELF-STUDY QUESTIONS

- What do I want to teach children about diversity (gender, sexual orientation, race, ethnicity, religion, abilities, and economic class)?

- What is my experience with these topics? What core beliefs do I have?

- What do I want to bring to my class to explore diversity and differing beliefs?

- What do I know about each child's experience?

- How can I individualize my teaching to celebrate the home culture of my families?

- How can I let other adults know that I celebrate differences in my classroom?

- What kinds of differences do my students point out?

- What are some things I can say to help them delight in differences?

- How can I help children feel safe and seen while including respect for their backgrounds?

- Do I have any activities, such as field trips or enrichment classes, that exclude any children? Do I have assistance to ensure all can take part?

- What can I say when a child or adult talks about difference in a way that hurts someone's feelings?

- What communication style(s) do I use?

- Do some of my families/children communicate differently than I do?

- How do I use body language to show people I respect them?

- What does my classroom media (posters, books, games, and so forth) show students about diversity and identity? How am I using these tools to support learning?

## Physical, Emotional, and Cognitive Diversity

Accommodating for physical and cognitive differences requires training, support, and sensitivity—it means meeting children "where they are at." All children deserve to be supported in all of the ways that make them unique. Each child is special. Each child is gifted.

Some children have physical, mental, emotional, and learning differences and disabilities that direct and define how we should meet their needs. At the YWCA, we advocate for a solid understanding of standards to help teachers reach children and to help parents understand developmental spectrums. Our educators work to view special interventions as opportunities for growth, not as negative consequences.

The best way to do that is to put a plan in place so teachers know what to do when they think a child needs extra support. With the help of ongoing observations, assessments, and screening tools, we can have clear, objective conversations about development with parents and outside service providers. We talk more about observation in chapter 6. Supporting children's needs is a multidimensional effort. For example, there are many professional observation and assessment tools, as well as district and other agency resources. Families are the primary resource for understanding their child's behaviors, needs, and experiences. Having systems in place such as home visits, conferences, or daily reports are an invaluable resource.

All children deserve to have their talents supported. When we are motivated to learn new caregiving techniques, our talents and expertise grow. The YWCA anti-bias curriculum advocates for working with families and specialists to help meet the needs of all children. Not only will children be happy and successful, but we will be too.

# Anti-Bias Education: Goals

We have previously mentioned the book *Anti-Bias Education for Young Children and Ourselves* (2010, 2020) by Louise Derman-Sparks and Julie Olsen Edwards. It is widely considered a standard for supporting anti-bias teaching in early childhood settings. According to Derman-Sparks and Olsen Edwards, the goals of anti-bias early childhood education are to support identity, diversity, justice, and activism. We appreciate their work and recognize it has strong ties to a social and emotional domain of development. We include the anti-bias goals developed by Derman-Sparks and Olsen Edwards here because we have found them to be successful guides:

## SELF-STUDY QUESTIONS

- When I think a student in my program needs special support, how do I feel?

- What personal and professional support do I need to be at my best?

- When I think students would benefit from special support, what is my process to get them what they need?

- How do I engage families in this process? How might they feel? How can I find out?

- What personal and professional support do families need to be at their best?

- How do I show students that I value their differences?

- What do I want to teach children about special abilities and needs?

- What is my experience with special abilities and needs? What core beliefs do I have?

- What do I know about each child's experience with this subject?

- How is the classroom environment playing into behaviors? How could it be changed to shift behaviors?

- How am I adjusting my expectations and building my lesson plan to meet the needs of the children?

- **Identity** goals include the development of self-awareness, confidence, family pride, and positive social identity.
- **Diversity** goals include expressing comfort and joy with human diversity, using accurate language for human differences, and creating deep, caring human connections.
- Our goals for **justice** are that learners will be able to increasingly recognize unfairness, have the language to describe unfairness, and understand that unfairness hurts.
- **Activism** goals call on young people to demonstrate empowerment and the skills to act, with others or alone, against prejudice and/or discriminatory actions.

What does it look like when we weave the goals of identity, diversity, justice, and activism into the daily life of the classroom? A great example is Ms. Kara's classroom sand exercise, in which she supported anti-bias learning.

Ms. Kara planned to make kinetic sand with her class. Marco and Elias helped her set up the activity. Her students smiled and talked as they used bowls, spoons, and eye-droppers to mix baking soda, baking powder, liquid soap, paint, and essential oils. Miss Kara realized this was an opportunity to honor and explore home culture.

"Where have you seen other kinds of sand?" she asked.

"The playground," said one student.

"My auntie's house!" said another.

"By the water!" said a third.

More students chimed in. Children started discussing who they were with when they visited sandy places. At first, the group directed their statements only to Ms. Kara, but once she got the ball rolling, the children started to talk to each other. Ms. Kara did not get in their way. When they began comparing the way their skin looked under the smears of sand, paint, oils, and soap, she smiled and encouraged more conversation about the many ways skin color can be different.

Suddenly, the play came to a halt.

"These are mine!" Elias announced, taking the mixing tools from his friends and collecting them at his spot. "I put them out!"

The other children looked to Ms. Kara. She smiled at them.

"Elias," she said, "I heard you say these tools are yours. Is that right?"

"Yes," said Elias.

"Elias, when you tell us these tools are yours, I don't think that's right. Do you know what I mean?"

"Yes, but I want this bowl and spoon. I need to have *all* of these so I can make a cake for my mom!"

"You need the bowl and spoon to make a cake? Is that right?" Ms. Kara asked.

"Yes, for my mom."

"What tool will you need after the bowl and spoon?"

"The flat pan," said Elias.

"Okay, what do you all think about laying the tools out in a line so we can use them in order?"

The group agreed on this solution. Together, they arranged the tools and placed them in a line. Later, they pretended they were in an operating room. The students became surgeons and assistants in a very serious procedure that lasted all the way to lunch.

With just a few minutes, some well-timed questions, and sensitive responses, Ms. Kara was able to raise her students' self-awareness. She celebrated their cultural and physical differences and social identities. She confronted unfairness and empowered her group to act against it.

In the next chapter, we talk about self-reflection and how it can help us understand ourselves, increase our sensitivity, and allow us to build stronger relationships with children and families.

## Chapter Point Summary

1. Anti-bias is the first principle of this curriculum. There is no effective conversation about best early childhood teaching or curriculum that does not bring the use of an anti-bias lens to the front of the conversation.

2. Areas of bias include gender, sexual orientation, race, ethnicity, culture, physical and cognitive abilities, religious beliefs, and economic and social status, just to name a few.

3. Communication styles are personal and cultural, and they can affect understanding or misunderstanding between people.

4. Culture shapes the way a person sees everything.

5. Developing an anti-bias teaching practice begins with self-reflection.

6. The four principles of anti-bias education can be addressed in everyday experiences with preschoolers.

# CHAPTER THREE
# Self-Reflective Practice

*How can I know myself better, to improve
my anti-bias teaching skills?*

When we refer to self-reflective practice, we are thinking of using self-knowledge as a tool for uncovering and addressing bias in order to achieve greater social justice and better educational outcomes for children. Ken Zeichner and Katrina Yan Liu (2010) remind educators to use a self-reflective practice in the name of social justice awareness. We agree. What is the point of teaching if not for social justice? What is the point of self-reflection if not for social justice? While it is important to think about how the technical aspects of teaching and learning happen in the classroom, it is unsupportive or worse if it is not accompanied by an explicit goal of social justice. We have long said that the best practice is anti-bias practice. Self-reflective skills can help people essentially know themselves in order to practice anti-bias teaching. Sometimes self-awareness leads to critical awareness. Critical awareness generally refers to being self-aware and then critically awareness of social systems and the ways people are privileged or marginalized within them. We do seek to use self-reflection as a tool toward greater understanding and for the eventual purpose of critical awareness, but to do so would require an additional volume. There is a difference between critical self-awareness, critical cultural-awareness, etc. We are starting with self-reflection because this is first step along the journey: examining what the self can do before applying it to the broader culture.

With that said, we think it suffices to say that a self-reflective practice helps us develop our self-awareness. It reminds us that we all see the world in slightly or dramatically different ways, depending on our lived experiences. As we move through life, we constantly draw from our own lived experiences to act and react. These experiences can be thought of as subtle or overt ways of knowing, and, generally speaking, they create our individual culture. This simply means our personal history or background information tells us how we should behave and interact with others.

The potentially negative thing about lived experiences is how they can limit our perspectives. But by questioning ourselves, we can learn to recognize how our lived experiences influence our interpretations, reactions, and beliefs. Melissa Tehee, Devon Isaacs, and Melanie Domenech Rodríguez (2020) explained that understanding cultures is a lifelong process—it is complex and takes a lot of effort. Louise Derman-Sparks, Debbie LeeKeenan, and John Nimmo (2015) advocate for the use of a self-reflective practice. Self-reflection is crucial and essential if we are to uncover, examine, and change biased behavior. By examining our lived experiences, we learn how our past has contributed to who we are today. This self-awareness can positively influence relationships with others, and the benefits extend into the classroom as well.

As with our overview of how we are thinking about bias, this chapter about self-reflection also is a brief overview of a deep body of research that is both nuanced and varied. This chapter explains how we think of using a self-reflective practice to support high-quality anti-bias teaching through play-based learning. A self-reflective practice can help us see ourselves and the world more clearly. It is a critical component of anti-bias work because it reminds educators that each person's perspective is crucial to support diversity. Each is special, and it is just one of many.

Self-reflection is an essential tool that promotes social justice and leads to more impactful teaching. With a self-reflective practice, we can begin to understand that all people use different perspectives that guide how they navigate the world. This helps us relate more authentically to our families and colleagues. We can build stronger friendships, and, according to Jessica Essary and Tunde Szecsi (2018) this can have a big effect on our professional lives. Friendships between colleagues can upend negative bias and reduce misconceptions about culture. Other researchers would agree that self-reflection makes us more effective in the classroom (Civitillo, Juang, and Schachner 2018; Zeichner and Liu 2010; Gay and Kirkland 2003). We wholeheartedly agree! We think this is one key to building an anti-bias environment.

As we learn to appreciate the cultural perspectives around us, anti-bias teachers must remember that students are developing into cultural beings. It is widely agreed that the foundation of a child's understanding of the world is the family. Herman Knopf and Kevin Swick (2008, 2007) suggest that being responsive to families can help reduce problems that occur when communication is low. Laura McFarland-Piazza and Rachel Saunders (2012) added to this with the affirmation that families and teachers in partnership can best support children. This kind of thinking can be traced to Urie Bronfenbrenner's ecological models of human development (Bronfenbrenner 1994; Thomas Weisner 2008).

In short, families are individual units that are part of a larger culture and early childhood teachers are also part of the cultural system. Teachers can dramatically affect child development as well. Each new life experience influences a child's personal culture, so as we help our students respond to the world, we guide their growth. Teachers walk a fine line. In order to authentically connect with families and individualize our teaching, we must regularly evaluate our own psychology.

Does this mean everything is relative? Should we withhold all of our judgments and ignore our principles? Absolutely not! Humans need to make judgments and connections. We just cannot let our judgments and connections become set in stone or harmful. Our communities are dynamic and changing, so our judgments and connections need to grow and change as well.

At the YWCA, we use self-reflection as a tool to evaluate our judgments. This helps us uncover our own biases and ensure that our community connections are responsive and socially responsible. We can judge our own judgments, using the goal of equality and equity as our standard. Most people have the best of intentions, but rigorous, honest self-reflection helps ensure we are acting in ways that contribute to the common good.

This is often difficult work. It can be uncomfortable, but at the YWCA, we remind ourselves that the best change happens when comfort zones are challenged (Riley and Solic 2017). One of our teachers told us that she knows she is learning when she feels like she knows nothing. It's risky to learn about ourselves and dig into our deep and underlying thoughts, and it can make people feel unstable and worried. Yet when we commit to this form of professional development, we build many things, including trusting relationships with families and colleagues, more equitable communities, and a more accurate sense of self.

At the YWCA, we found that the teachers who commit to a self-reflective practice often find themselves less frustrated and burned out. They can solve problems more easily. The wisdom they cultivate allows them to respect their students' perspectives, enjoy their talents, and better support their behaviors. This leads to greater job satisfaction and more individualized teaching.

There are many ways to be self-reflective. Some questions that help us reflect and check for personal bias include the following:

- Why am I bringing this experience to the class?
- What do I want to teach?
- What is my experience with this subject? What core beliefs do I have?
- What do I know about each child's experience?
- Who benefits from my actions or perspectives?

We can also practice a number of exercises to dig into our own identities and discover what sorts of assumptions we make about the world. Try this:

Close your eyes. Think about a student in your classroom. Imagine that student at home. Imagine the furniture, the colors, the smells, and the sounds. Ask yourself: Why did I picture my student's home this way? Why did I form these assumptions about my student's home life?

As this exercise demonstrates, a powerful benefit of self-reflection is that we can notice the fabricated beliefs we have about the people around us. We make assumptions all the time, often without realizing what we are doing. We can evaluate how these assumptions lead to expectations, labels, and misinterpretations.

Anti-bias self-reflective work is a lifelong, life-changing process. It is a good thing that teachers are lifelong learners!

Here are seven more self-reflective exercises. We recommend working on these with a partner or group. It is always beneficial to work with others, especially when one of our goals is to see and understand other people's perspectives and lived experiences. After trying these activities, one teacher said the biggest thing she learned was that all teachers have their own perspectives. Her idea of how to enact best practices does not have to be the only idea. Throughout this section, we share more of our stories to show how these practices have affected some of our teachers. We hope these exercises help you create a professional learning community committed to developing an anti-bias lens.

## Self-Reflective Exercise #1: Earliest Memories

This is a self-reflective exercise that should be practiced in the context of a safe, professional development setting. Depending on a person's personal history, and while there is no right or wrong answer, these questions might be triggering. The facilitator should ensure people can feel safe to explore what comes up for them, including the history and trauma that comes along with these questions. Group members should be reminded that no one can tell a person's background or experiences simply by looking at them.

Answer the questions:

- Where are you from?
- List what you remember about your birthplace, or the place that identify with most from your childhood.
- What was the first time you can remember becoming aware of race, class, or gender (depending on the reflection topic) from before you were ten years old?
- At the time, how did you feel?
- As a child, what did you dream about becoming or doing when you grew up?
- Who were your teachers, mentors, or heroes?
- List your memories of being aware race, class, or gender between the ages of 11–18.
- At the time, how did you feel?
- When and how did you become aware of race, class, or gender on the national or global level?
- What did the media tell you?

- What did you learn from conversations in your community?
- What did you want to do when you heard/saw/discovered these messages?
- List your experiences of race, class, or gender when you became 18-years-old or older.

We hypothesize that the things we learned in our earliest memories of play influence the ways we teach young children.

One of our teachers, Ms. Angie, found that this exercise was a useful way to begin her anti-bias, self-reflective practice. She clearly remembered learning how to ride a bicycle by herself. She fell and scraped up her knees. Rather than give up, she went home and found foam sponges to tape onto her knees, so that when she fell again it would hurt less. Ms. Angie said, "Today I see myself as a person who looks for the solution to every problem. Then I take action."

Ms. Kane said she becomes frustrated when children in her classroom are not willing to try new activities. She explained that as a child she was paralyzed, and she walks today by her force of will. Her memory of play is unique to her, and because of it she thinks all children are capable of achieving anything they put their minds to. However, once she was able to see how her experience limited her perspective, she decided to be more sensitive to her students' reservations and fears.

## Self-Reflective Exercise #2 (Version 1): I Am From

- Where are you from?
- List what you remember about your birthplace.
- List your memories of race, class, or gender from before you were ten years old.
- At the time, how did you feel?
- What did you dream about becoming or doing as a child?
- Who were your teachers, mentors, or heroes?
- List your middle and high school memories of race, ethnicity, class, or gender.
- At the time, how did you feel?
- List what you knew about race, ethnicity, class, or gender on the national or global level when you were a teen.
- What did the media tell you?
- What did you learn from conversations in your community?
- What did you want to do when you heard/saw/discovered these messages?
- List your experiences of race, class, or gender when you became an adult.

- How do these memories make you feel?
- Rewrite each answer. Use your answers to finish the phrase, "I am from."

YWCA teacher Esther found that transforming her memories about racism into a poem gave her the opportunity to look at her life more objectively. This template allowed her to express some difficult moments that she would not normally think or talk about. Here is what she wrote:

*I am from South Minneapolis.*

*I am from bike trips to Powderhorn Park, huge families moving in and out of the apartment building next door, and buying Big Chew at the gas station on the corner.*

*I am from brown and white people mixed together at church and in our neighborhood, but worrying when my dad, my brother, and I were the only black faces everywhere else. Getting a snack after school at my Hmong neighbor's house and not being able to read the packaging on the bright bags in the cupboard. My grandmother telling my mom to do something about my hair.*

*I am from feeling worried and very aware of when I fit in and when I didn't.*

*I am from wanting to be a famous movie star.*

*I am from children's theater people who put us in shows, my grandmother who gave me confidence, my mom who drove me everywhere and cheered me on.*

*I am from wearing Rodney King T-shirts to school and being the only person who knew who Tracey Chapman was.*

*I am from being the only one. The Exotic. I am from feeling special, then fraudulent, then, ashamed.*

*I am from hearing stories from my dad about police brutality and discrimination.*

*I am from praying I would wake up and look like Kimberly from* Different Strokes. *Nobody looked like me on TV.*

*I am from a theater group that thought kids could make a difference if we spoke up. We travelled to other high schools. I was a star.*

*I am from wanting to make a difference like my dad, but law school seemed so boring. With preschoolers I could sing, dance, read books, and change the world.*

## Self-Reflective Exercise #2 (Version 2): I Am From

This is a self-reflective essay that should be practiced in the context of a safe, professional development setting. Depending on a person's personal history, and while there are no right or wrong answers, these questions might be trigger. These questions should be answered in relation to a specific topic, such as a first memory of school or the topic of safety or playing. The facilitator should ensure people can feel safe to explore what comes up for the them, including the history and trauma that comes along with these questions.

Group members should be reminded that no one can tell a person's background or experiences simply by looking at them.

Answer the following questions:

- What did you hear the most as a young child under the age of ten?
- Where did you go that was special for you and your family?
- What smells do you associate with that memory?
- What did you think when you were there?
- Are there other smells, sights, or sounds that stand out to you?
- What did you think about yourself as a result of this experience?
- Use the answers to finish the phrase, "I am from."

Ms. Dianne, a teacher from the YWCA, did the exercise and shared it with a group of colleagues. She read:

*I am from my mom telling me to "make a list of what is good and bad, make your decision based on that," and "we can only make choices with the information we have and not be angry with ourselves later."*

*I am from my father saying: "I'd give you a gift but I don't know what you like." From my mother again, "Don't keep it inside" and making up songs until we cried, laughing.*

*I am from my mother loving cooking and making art with my brother and sister.*

*I am from my neighborhood . . . singing as loud as I could . . . walking in the warm night to my best friend's house.*

*I am from the happiest and best family, my cousins, my grandparents, my uncles, and aunties, all whom I loved blindly.*

*I am from watching my mother tuck her hair behind her ear in the car and thinking she was the most beautiful person on earth.*

*I am from the cabin, racing through the woods and swimming, putting on plays, eating raspberry tarts and fried fish with Grandma and Auntie.*

*I am from camp with the smell of horses and the freedom to be me.*

*I am from a world where I could be anything I wanted because my mom told me I could.*

After Ms. Dianne had a chance to hear poems by her colleagues, she said she really appreciated the individuality each teacher brought to their teams. She also thought deeply about her teaching decisions. With new insight, she noticed how her culture affected the kinds of learning experiences she valued and offered to her students.

"I thought it was just my instincts that made me do a lot of cooking, singing, arts, plays, and crafts with my class," she reported. "I think now it might be because that is how I was raised."

She continued, "I think my mom's trust in me is part of why I trust children so much. I work really hard to let [my students] make their own decisions as much as possible. [My mother] put everything she had behind all of us." She also said her idealized understanding of childhood had become more complicated as she grew. Knowing it was her instinct to accept her family unconditionally made her wonder how all children experience family.

Ms. Libby, another YWCA teacher, added to the conversation. "I thought my dad was a superhero," she said. "Whenever he was gone my mom would say he was saving baby animals in an oil spill or rescuing people. It wasn't until I was much older that I learned he was in jail. I'm still a daddy's girl."

"We never know which experiences will be the ones that stick [with our students] when they are grown," Ms. Rae concluded. "It's our job to make each moment as good as it can be."

This exercise also helped teachers investigate how the role models they had, or lacked, as children informed the expectations they placed on themselves and projected on the students and adults in their lives.

According to Ms. Shaeron, "As a child, I was playing a lot with my cousins. We had arguments, and they were not always small. I learned that I was competent early on. My mom was a young woman in the '60s. She saw civil rights; she was pre–Title IX and saw that change. She drilled it into me that I could be anything at all that I wanted to be. She always told me that I was unstoppable."

Ms. Mica said, "I didn't grow up with an active or present father. I have a hard time understanding or imagining a home like that. I notice now that I feel mistrustful and uncertain with fathers. I really need to work on that."

# Self-Reflective Exercise #3: Communication Styles

There are many styles of communicating and ranges of preferences that include but are not limited to personal space, smiling, eye contact, touch, and silence. People using different communication styles can misunderstand each other and misread body language. Fortunately, we can cultivate an awareness of how we communicate and how this can affect the people around us. At the YWCA, we use self-reflection to explore our communication styles and preferences. Below are some communication concepts to help you get started with your own reflection.

## Personal space

Some people do not like to be close to others when they talk. Do you or do you not? Why? Watch others and try to see if you can be sensitive to the needs of others for personal space. Can you ask people what they prefer? Can you share your preferences?

## Smiling

Do you say you are fine when you are not? Why or why not? How does this affect your professional teaching life? How does this affect your friendships? What can you learn about others and how they use smiles?

## Eye contact

Have you ever tried to get the eye of a person who did not love deep eye contact? Have you ever had someone try to catch your eye and it felt awkward or even threatening? Why or why not? What can you find out about others and their thoughts and feelings about eye contact? YWCA co-teachers Ms. Ada and Ms. Dianne had differing communication styles that made it difficult for them to build a trusting relationship with each other. Too much eye contact made Ms. Ada suspicious. "I think she is trying to see if I'm doing something wrong," she reported.

"I'm trying to show her that I really care about her and this work, but she won't even look me in the eye!" Ms. Dianne explained.

With some guided self-reflection, Ms. Ada and Ms. Dianne were able to identify their own biases and discover some important personal and cultural differences about each other. These exercises brought them relief and understanding. It helped them become a better team.

## Touch

What does touching someone say about you? What does it say to others? How can you find out if you are being both respectful to others and aware of your physical space concepts?

## Speaking and listening

If you were to think of what a stereotypical image of a classroom is, we think the chances are high that you will imagine a teacher talking in front of quiet students, some of whom have raised hands to offer the "correct" answer. Christina Davidson and Chris Edwards-Groves (2020) produced a study focused on the ways teachers use recitation in early childhood settings. The expectation is that a child will correctly repeat the answer only when asked. They further explained how pervasive the assumption is that when a teacher speaks, children are to listen. We have noticed this as well. We have noticed that some teachers think they are to occupy a place of authority that is unfairly advantaged over others who are not teachers. We have noticed that teachers who think they should dominate the conversation have tired voices at the end of the day and are frustrated by children who "won't listen." We have noticed some family members are very nervous when speaking to teachers as if somehow their child's teacher could somehow "fail" their child.

There is much research on conversation meaning, patterns, style, and uses, but as with our other topics, we want to think about speaking and listening in terms of how our individual bias may affect the ways we listen to and speak with others. One way we introduce this concept from an anti-bias perspective is to ask teachers to consider how speaking and listening patterns can come in many styles. Some people overlap when talking to show how excited they are to contribute to the conversation. Some people are uncomfortable if more than a second or two goes by in a conversation—they have a thought or comment at the ready to prove they are listening and engaged. Still others listen to a speaker with full force, then pause before responding, sometimes taking up to ten seconds to figure out what they want to say. Take a moment to think about your personal communication habits. What kind of a listener and speaker are you? Why? With whom does this conflict? How can you find out more about other people's speaking and listening patterns? We are not trying to take a specific position on whether there is a right or wrong way of speaking and listening. We want to consider the variety of ways people communicate that intersect across cultures and identities.

## Time concepts

Robert Levine (2015) has offered ways to consider how concepts of time can differ between people and across cultures. There is a large canon of research devoted to how time is used and perceived within and throughout people's lives, from corporations to countries. You might be wondering what concepts of time have to do with how we communicate. Many people feel that timeliness sends a message. People who love to schedule activities may think of time as fixed and finite. They might make a plan to show how much they care about the things that need to be done. Others view time as a series of chances. Time is a moving thing that can come back around. People like this might think of time as infinite and show high levels of caring by being extremely flexible with their schedule, especially their free time. A search on the internet today for "concepts of time" will open up an array of thoughts that relate to the ways time is portrayed, researched, and used. We like to think about the ways people use time from a position of equity. Is time a luxury, and if so, whose? Whose notion of "correct" time is privileged? This section is not sufficient to address all of the ways time can intersect with histories of disenfranchisement, culture, and time, but should serve as a thought exercise for teachers to explore how they measure time and have expectations around how time should be used.

Imagine if two teachers on each end of the spectrum of time preferences worked together. One might say, "Why are you always so concerned about following this schedule? The students are having fun—let's just keep doing this." Or, "Yesterday I noticed that the kids get too antsy to sit for circle time before pickup. I think we should change our plan."

The other teacher might say, "We have to follow this plan for both the daily schedule and the lesson plan. People need to know exactly what to expect and when to expect it." No one perspective is correct. The question is whose version of usage of time was being privileged and why?

## Addressing communication styles up front

Barbara Curbow and colleagues (2000) used a rating system to measure what causes stress for ECE teachers. They found that misunderstandings between parents and teachers are a common stressor. Teachers of young children say miscommunication between themselves and parents hinders their ability to best support children. When teachers let parents know what kind of communicator they are, this is an opportunity to make a communication plan that is supportive of all parties. This sharing can open the door to conversations that explore parents' preferences. This is one way to help avoid future miscommunication.

Here is an example of what a teacher might say during an intake meeting to bridge stylistic differences in communication:

"I want you to know that when I communicate with you, I have your and your child's interests at heart. One thing I know about myself is that I tend to be more of a nonverbal communicator. I learned this from my family. I am from Somalia, and my culture taught me to defer to my elders. I tend to look down when I am in conversations with people. Since I view you as an authority, I might not make a lot of direct eye contact with you. I hope you understand that this is a sign of respect for me. What kind of a communicator are you? How do you feel most comfortable? I think it is very important that we share this kind of information so we have the best relationship possible. It will help your child feel more comfortable with me in class."

You can make your own script using the following template:

"I want you to know that when I communicate with you, I have your and your child's interests at heart. One thing I know about myself as a communicator is that I tend to _____. I learned this from my family. I am from _____ and my culture taught me to (describe one or two examples of your communication style) _____ _____. What kind of a communicator are you? How do you feel most comfortable? I think it is very important that we share this kind of information so we have the best relationship possible. It will help your child feel more comfortable with me in class."

## Self-Reflective Exercise #4: Windows and Doors

Materials: Paper, magazines to be cut up, scissors, and glue

Step 1: Teachers fold their sheet of paper in half.

Step 2: The front of the paper symbolizes a façade or a "door." Teachers cut out and glue images here that show

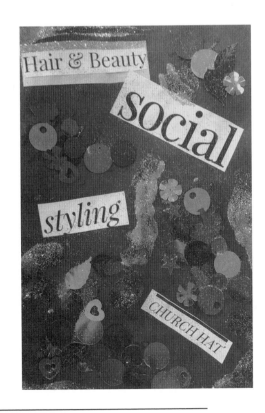

- what they put "up front," or the image they project to the world
- how they want to be seen
- how they are perceived by others

Step 3: Inside the paper is the inner self. Teachers cut out and glue images here that show things others cannot tell about them just by looking.

Step 4: Teachers talk about what is on their front "doors" with a group of peers.

Step 5: Teachers share what is on the inside. Some teachers may choose to cut windows to show some of the inside; others might open the whole door to share what is inside.

Questions for reflection in this activity include the following:

- Do people see me the way I want to be seen?
- Do I see others the way they want to be seen?
- Did I open the door to share what is inside? Did I add a window? Why or why not?
- What is inside that I could bring out to let people know me better?
- What do I think I see on the "doors" of families and children?
- What might be behind a family's "doors"? How can I find out?

This activity led Ms. Yassin to consider being more open about who she is on the inside. "I've been hoping people can see who I am," she said, "but talking in this group makes me realize people don't really know what kind of person I am unless I tell them."

## Self-Reflective Exercise #5: Examining Personal Bias

Make a table. In one column, write topics including—but not limited to—Personal Bias, Stereotypes, Prejudice, Discrimination, and Microaggression. In another column, reflect on how these topics affect you, your students, their families, your communities, and other teachers. This table is an opportunity for you to organize and collect your thoughts. Once you've completed your table, discuss with your team or a trusted friend.

| | IMPACT ON SELF | IMPACT ON CHILDREN | IMPACT ON FAMILIES | IMPACT ON COMMUNITIES | IMPACT ON COLLEAGUES |
|---|---|---|---|---|---|
| **Personal Bias** | | | | | |
| **Stereotypes** | | | | | |
| **Prejudice** | | | | | |
| **Discrimination** | | | | | |
| **Microaggression** | | | | | |

Please remember, if you are a white person, it is not a person of color's job to help you work through your racial bias. Similarly, it is not a woman's responsibility to teach men how to examine their personal relationship with sexism and white patriarchy. This concept can be transferred to all individual differences. And, it is everyone's responsibility to take action. All people can develop a working self-awareness that helps them stop negative bias from hurting others. But we are not discouraging talking with others. For example, we have found sharing with others in a safe teacher-development setting helps people address their own concerns and receive support from willing and multiple perspectives.

## Self-Reflective Exercise #6: Triggers

We all have triggers. For example, if someone contradicts one of our beliefs, we may feel irritated, angry, or afraid. Our self-reflective practice can help us determine when the triggered belief is biased. Often, our biases make us feel that we know better about what is good for our students than their family or another teacher.

What has triggered you lately? You can use the mind-map diagram below to help you think about why you are reacting to any particular situation. Can you find root causes of your thoughts, feelings, or actions that may be linked to unconscious bias? If you want to change the outcomes, try changing your thinking and try something new. Here is one teacher's example of a bias that triggered very negative feelings and made it difficult for her to connect with a parent.

Ms. Alma used to be very judgmental toward a parent who stayed home during the day. However, "Thinking back now," she said, "I can see so many negative messages I was sending—there is so much to this." Alma said the mind map helped her see how what she thought might not be the way the parent saw things. "I have to remember, we are all trying to do what is best for this child, and parents and guardians have a lot to juggle too. I don't always know why choices are made, and in the meantime I need to focus on making each day as safe and fun as possible." Teacher Liz added that one of the toughest situations for her is when a parent becomes angry when a child is ill or injured while in her care. She reflected, "When I ask myself if the parent is angry because they love or don't love their child it helps me calm down. I also was thinking this parent was blaming me because they thought I didn't care or wasn't careful enough. That made me angry because I'm here every day and it is because I care that I do this work. I will work on not taking it personally because I know how much I care. When a parent is upset I will keep doing my best to keep calm."

In this activity, as you explore the "Thoughts" and "Feelings" bubbles, keep asking yourself why, and why again, until you reach back as far back as you can remember to find the root of your thoughts in your past experiences.

## Mind Map

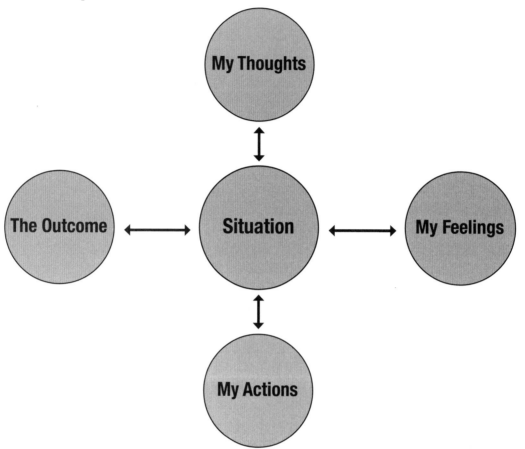

## Self-Reflective Exercise #7: Unique Abilities

This is a great icebreaker or hands-on activity for a group of teachers that can be easily incorporated into a group setting.

Materials: A variety of recycled and/or open-ended art supplies.

Goals include the following:

- to recognize our skills and abilities as well as one another's
- to get to know one another better
- to deepen our knowledge of open-ended play
- to practice positive encouragement and realize the power of asking questions

The group uses the materials to create an open-ended art activity. After the creative time is over, perhaps 30 minutes, teachers take turns sharing their work. The sharing teacher uses this guide.

When I made this art . . .

- "I was thinking about _____."
- "I was feeling _____."

- Plus anything else the person would like to add

The teachers who are listening can practice giving positive feedback that celebrates the work of each individual. They reflect on the ways in which each teacher shows individual skills and abilities.

Teachers reflect on the following questions about their own experience:

- In what way did having free time to create help me strengthen my skills and abilities?
- How did I feel when the time for creating was over? Why?
- How did I feel when I received encouragement? Why?
- How did I feel when asked questions? Why?
- How will this experience help me in my work with my class?

Asking questions and commenting on the work and effort helps people get to know each other and themselves better. When we know each other, we can be less judgmental and more supportive of our differences.

We hope these exercises lay a positive and fruitful foundation for a self-reflective practice. Remember, teachers' ways of thinking, behaving, and being are influenced by their cultures—just as the ways of children and families are influenced by theirs (Krasnoff 2016; McFarland-Piazza and Saunders 2012). Teachers' home cultures may be very different from those of the children in their classrooms.

Teachers' individual experiences shape how they see children. Fabienne Doucet (2017) says that what teachers believe about children shapes the way teachers think and feel about the children, and that affects children's successes. For teachers who are anti-bias, to increase effectiveness in their classrooms, they look beyond personalized cultural lenses. From there, they also try to understand how children interpret the world differently because of their personalized cultural beliefs.

It is important to recognize that respecting other people's cultures does not diminish one's own. In chapter 4, we focus on using an expanded cultural perspective to build relationships with the most important people in a child's life—family.

## Chapter Point Summary

1. Each person is an individual. We each have our own culture with specific sources of knowledge that define our social and cognitive field of vision. It is normal to form systems of understanding and make judgments. Self-reflection can help us become aware of this behavior, and it helps strengthen and protect us—and those around us—from negative bias.
2. A self-reflective anti-bias practice is a highly professional commitment.
3. Having bias does not mean a teacher does not care; working to unravel bias shows how much a teacher cares.
4. You can begin your self-reflective study by understanding your personal identity. This is just the beginning—anti-bias work is a lifelong commitment.

# CHAPTER FOUR
# Families: The World of Children

## *How can I connect with families to help children learn?*

It is common for teachers to use the terms parents and families when discussing the loved ones in a child's life, when in reality a "parent" might be a guardian or caregiver. Use of the word "parent" inherently implies a white, heterosexual, married couple, as opposed to using language to refer to the primary guardian of the child. Families can include the people with whom children and parents or guardians spend their daily lives. This is an opportunity for growth across the field. We believe that early childhood educators know a lot about children in general, while families are the number one authorities on their own child. It is the ethical responsibility of teachers to support children and their families. We are supported by the position statements of the National Association for the Education of Young Children (NAEYC); clear statements of best practices such as these are structurally valuable to our work as anti-bias educators. For example, the Advancing Equity in Early Childhood Education position statement outlines important ways that anti-bias work is supported through deep respect of families (NAEYC 2019). A child's value is expressed through the ways teachers connect with and respect the children's families. We agree, and the research backs it up: children have the best chance for success in a learning environment where there is an honest, committed partnership between teachers and families.

    This chapter focuses on some ways an anti-bias framework can help build stronger partnerships with families. As with previous chapters, this is again an overview of a very comprehensive body of research, and we have chosen to highlight some of the concepts most important to us. As with each of these chapters on bias, our approach is one of many ways to view and practice excellent anti-bias early childhood education.

## Families Matter

One goal of anti-bias teaching is to nurture the identity and self-esteem of each student. Since children develop their cultural and individual identities at home, it is important that we connect with their families (Douglass and Gittell 2012; Fenton,

Ocasio-Stoutenburg, and Harry 2017; Gonazales-Mena 2008; NAEYC 2019). Bonding with parents also has academic benefits. According to YWCA teacher Mr. Robert, "Positive relationships with parents can help us understand where to meet children on their social, emotional, and cognitive levels." The research agrees: solid partnerships between parents and teachers support children's best learning outcomes.

Recognizing and nurturing the individuality of families is especially important when working with marginalized groups. There are a variety of marginalized groups in the United States. As an example, gay and lesbian couples with adopted children experience intersectional marginalization. Abbie Goldberg and colleagues (2017) recognize that these families deserve explicit strategies for inclusion because of historical homophobic marginalization as well as the stigma of adoption. As another example and on the same note, Debra Ren-Etta Sullivan's (2016) work explains that families of Black children also deserve intentional inclusion because of the harmful effects of racism on a child's life. The need to carefully respect the differences among typically marginalized groups cannot be overstated.

Teachers who seek to recognize the uniqueness of all families can show respect and build relationships that support healthy growth and development between themselves and families. As one YWCA teacher said, "We are careful to include all ways of being a family. Children in our centers are biracial, multicultural, adopted, have same-sex parents, and some are of very low income." This careful inclusion thwarts a powerful stereotype that we have all been exposed to: the myth of the "traditional family." In stereotypical "traditional families," parents are typically white, married, reasonably wealthy, and heterosexual. Families who do not fit this mold get the message that they are abnormal and less valuable. An anti-bias lens can help us evaluate beliefs and media that uphold this stereotype. We can contradict them with images, activities, and stories that celebrate the diverse families in our communities.

When we work to understand the beliefs that guide children and their families, we become more culturally sensitive. This sensitivity allows us to understand the real lived experiences of the families and children we serve— and the effects of these experiences on development and learning. In order to do this, we have to step outside of our own cultural expectations about how families should look and behave. YWCA teacher Ms. Becca explains: "My definition and experience of family might be very different from the children and families in my class; I have to

accept and respect all families." This is not always easy.

In turn, we have found that families often have different visions from teachers about what is important for their child's well-being. For example, we have worked with parents who want their children to show the utmost obedience to adults, whereas a teacher might prefer the students to openly share what is on their mind. Parents may also use different methods to support their children in reaching their goals. A teacher might give a group of children extra time to get their coats on by themselves while a parent might take over the zipping and snapping. It is likely that both caregivers have valid reasons for supporting children in these conflicting ways. The more we can communicate about why we do things the way we do, the more we can appreciate the feelings, beliefs, and needs that drive these differences. These conversations work best between partners who trust and care about each other. So, how do we create those bonds?

One way to build common ground is to move out of our comfort zones and to take part in the community and cultural events that the families in our classroom find meaningful. Here is a story from a normally shy YWCA teacher, Ms. Carla, who took on this challenge.

Several classroom parents told Ms. Carla about an annual community festival. Some of the parents asked Ms. Carla if she was going to be there; they thought she would have fun. At first, she hesitated. "I didn't live in their neighborhood," she said. She thought she might be uncomfortable at the festival, not living in the community and not knowing many people.

But she changed her mind and decided to go. The reward for her bravery was a wonderful experience that offered her valuable new perspectives. "I had so much fun listening to the bands, watching the dancers, and seeing the different booths," she reported. She also saw many of her students' families—all of whom were very happy to see her and spend time with her.

The following Monday, as Ms. Carla greeted children and families arriving at school, the children she saw at the festival all talked about how excited they were that she had come. She thought about how good it was to see some of her families outside of the familiar preschool setting. She was able to get to know them a little bit better—and they had gotten to know her better as well.

Ms. Carla reflected, "This was worth doing. I got closer to families and children—I can see more now. I think the parents really liked it that I was there, and I loved being there. We played 'festival' that week in the dramatic play area. I think there is a way to make it part of next week's lesson plan too."

We know this story is a common one—when teachers bring themselves to events in their students' communities, it changes the relationship between families and teachers.

---

## SELF-STUDY QUESTIONS

- What kinds of activities do I imagine my families might enjoy?

- Why did I form those assumptions about their lives?

- How can I find out about community events that matter to my families?

- Would my presence there be appreciated? How can I find out?

- Does my classroom media (posters, books, games, and so forth) celebrate activities that connect to the home cultures of my families?

---

## Goals for Relationships with Families

These are the four YWCA anti-bias curriculum goals for relationships between teachers and families:

1. Recognize and respect one another's knowledge and expertise; share power and decision-making.
2. Create networks of support.
3. Acknowledge and respect culture.
4. Share information through two-way communication.

We next describe how teachers work toward achieving these goals.

### Goal one: Recognize and respect one another's knowledge and expertise; share power and decision-making

Building effective family-centered partnerships means using the expertise of families and teachers both. Early childhood professionals have long acknowledged that parents are a child's primary educators; families teach their children what they know about life. Unsurprisingly, parents are experts on the individual children they bring to our classroom. We teachers, on the other hand, offer helpful information about child development and best practices that is applicable to every child. When families and teachers work together, our training and professional experience can help them navigate the preschool years more easily.

Making sure everyone is on the same page can be challenging; this is true in many areas of life. This is especially difficult if a parent or teacher is struggling to communicate. On a large scale, Suejung Han (2017) found that personal insecurity can inhibit people's ability to trust others whom they perceive to be different from them. We think this means some parents or caregivers might be reluctant, or unable, to express what they know about their child's development. Similarly, some teachers may be too shy to share what they know about child development. It is ultimately the teacher's responsibility to overcome the fear, insecurity, or hesitation in order to promote open communication with parents.

Getting to know the families involved in a child's care is a delicate balance of give and take. We have come to believe that teachers practicing anti-bias and self-refection should avoid trying to "educate" families because that can lower a parent's confidence. On the flip side, teachers may feel intimidated when it seems they are not seeing eye-to-eye with a parent. It is helpful to keep the goals you have set together front and center. This became clear for one YWCA teacher when she realized that a student needed extra support. Here is her story.

Ms. Brandi was worried about one of her students. "Jacob won't follow along," she said. "I think it's something that needs looking into."

However, she had a hard time communicating her concerns with Jacob's mom, Mona. "Whenever I try to talk to Mona about Jacob, she won't listen. I've been recommending an assessment, and she's not interested. She says he's fine and I just don't see it." Ms. Brandi hoped setting up a meeting with Mona would allow her to discuss her observations and be taken seriously.

When Mona heard Ms. Brandi's concerns, she shared that she was working with Jacob at home and had seen several improvements in his behavior. For example, Mona learned she needed to touch Jacob's shoulder before she spoke to him if she wanted to get his full attention.

After their discussion, Ms. Brandi realized she had unfairly been making assumptions about Mona, and she incorporated Mona's suggestion in the classroom. Although Ms. Brandi did make progress in her efforts to get Jacob's full attention, she still felt there was a need for an assessment, and she decided to revisit the topic with Mona.

Ms. Brandi reflected, "I talked with her, and so did other teachers. His mom wanted the best for him, and maybe she was scared of an assessment. I told her I've seen [other] parents feel that way too and that an assessment could help Jacob thrive even more."

In order to help Mona feel supported, Ms. Brandi described the experiences of other families who had opted for an assessment. She hoped their successes would help Mona feel more confident about getting help. After several months, Mona agreed to an assessment. The assessment revealed that Jacob had hearing issues, and as a result, he was able to get the support he needed.

Ms. Brandi's decision to work on her bias—*Mona is not interested*—and foster open communication paid off. When asked about her partnership with Mona, Ms. Brandi said, "We now talk about ways to help Jacob communicate his thoughts more. Being on the same page has really changed our relationship. She knows I care about him too."

Teachers like Ms. Brandi who overcome their bias and gain the trust of parents receive something even more precious: more effective teaching relationships with their students.

Not all parents will automatically be interested in building a relationship with their children's teachers. Some may need encouragement. Parents' past school experiences can influence their present interactions with educators. One YWCA teacher needed to reach out in all kinds of ways before making a successful connection. Here is Ms. Mica's story.

Bryce was new to the classroom, and he was adjusting quickly. He had made friends with a few of the other children. Ms. Mica couldn't wait to tell Tamar, his mother. Ms. Mica had so many positive things she wanted to share with Bryce's parents, but despite her best efforts, they had not met since his orientation.

Ms. Mica liked to communicate with her class's families on a regular basis. In an attempt to reach Bryce's mother, she had left notes in Bryce's backpack, made telephone calls, and tried to speak with her at drop-off and pickup times. Tamar had not responded to the notes or the calls, and she always seemed to be in a hurry at drop-off and pickup.

One day during pickup, Tamar and Bryce had to wait for a rainstorm to subside a bit before making their way to the car. Ms. Mica noticed them in the doorway. She seized the opportunity to talk with Tamar.

"It's raining really hard out there, isn't it?" Ms. Mica said.

Tamar nodded her head.

"Did you see my note about how much fun Bryce had leading the group-time song yesterday?" Ms. Mica continued, "I put it in his backpack. Bryce is doing so well in class."

"I've been getting your notes and I think you might have left me a message. I don't really check voice mail," Tamar replied.

"Oh, that's okay," said Ms. Mica. "Bryce, did you tell your mom what song you chose yesterday?"

"The car song," said Bryce.

"Oh, he loves his cars," said Tamar.

Ms. Mica smiled. "I know," she said. "I want you to know we love having Bryce in our classroom."

Ms. Mica continued, "Bryce, were you in the block area and painting today?"

Bryce, who was listening to the conversation intently while watching the rain, nodded.

"He is so funny too! I'm trying to remember the joke he made today. We were all laughing so hard!"

Tamar looked at Bryce and said, "Yes, he is funny. He is always making me laugh. And he has colors at home and is always drawing some kind of picture for me."

"I bet so," Ms. Mica said. She smiled at Tamar and Bryce. "Well, I'd better go clean up our room. Next week there will be a sign-up sheet for conferences. I'll have some more stories for you then. I want to know what you want Bryce to be learning. Kindergarten is right around the corner!"

Tamar sighed and smiled back. "I hear that," she said. "I'll look for the sheet. Thanks."

"Great!" replied Ms. Mica. "Can't wait to see you tomorrow, Bryce!" Ms. Mica held the door open and high-fived Bryce as he and his mom left the center.

In their study, Herman Knopf and Kevin Swick (2007) share research that points to some things early childhood teachers can do to build an effective teacher-parent relationship. They remind us that there are many expectations and misconceptions parents and teachers can have about each other. Parents' past experiences with their own education, for example, may affect the relationship they have with their children's teachers. We wondered whether it might be more challenging to build a healthy relationship with teachers if parents' past educational experiences were negative. In our research, we found that about half of our teachers' first memories about school were not positive. This could be the same for your center's families. Like Ms. Mica, we all might have to try different strategies to

## SELF-STUDY QUESTIONS

- How can I gather positive stories throughout the day to share with parents?

- How many different ways can I use to communicate with families?

- Do I know all of my parents' names? How do they prefer to be addressed?

- What kind of support is available for families in my community?

- How do I let families know that I will partner with them?

When you think a child needs help, work through these questions:

- What does the parent do at home that may work well at the center?

- What up-to-date resources and studies are available to help me refine my approach?

- How is this situation making me feel?

- How is this situation making the child feel?

- How is this situation making the parent feel?

- What will success look like for everybody involved?

connect with some parents. Once we do, we have the chance to help them create memories that are more positive. Do not give up!

Like much of the research we have cited, we think for a partnership to be effective, teachers and families need to work together to set goals and make decisions. Shared power means shared input. When families and teachers work together, each party offers different perspectives on the situation, which ultimately leads to a more well-rounded approach.

## Goal two: Create networks of support

Families face many challenges in their efforts to raise happy, healthy children. Parents who build strong networks often get the support they need. A network is a system of connections and relationships that provide information and help to one another.

One of the best resources a parent can have is other parents. Teachers can create open communication channels, giving families opportunities to share information with one another and learn what resources are available in the larger community. Just as we introduce new children to their classmates, we can take time to introduce new parents to other families during drop-off and pickup.

When appropriate, we can help families connect over things they have in common. One YWCA teacher, Ms. Lynn, found a way to give parents an opportunity to connect and share resources. Here is her story.

Ms. Lynn's classroom was in charge of decorating one of the bulletin boards in the center hallway. One year, she decided to try something new. In a letter she sent home with the children, she explained that instead of decorating the bulletin board, it would be available for families to share resources, community events, and announcements. Families would be responsible for their postings and for removing postings when they became outdated or after a three-week period—whichever came first. If parents were interested in a particular posting, they could ask Ms. Lynn to make a copy of it for them.

Soon, the bulletin board was covered with valuable information. Parents learned about free computer classes and nearby garage sales. Ms. Lynn noticed that families often stopped by the board to see what was new.

She also noticed the board sparked conversations between people. One day, parents picking up their children noticed information about an open house at the local elementary school. They began to talk about things they were planning to buy for their children before they moved on to kindergarten.

"Afra should have a new backpack since it's almost time for kindergarten," said one parent.

"I just saw a sale at the store on the corner. They looked cute and weren't too expensive," said the other. They chatted about planning for the new year and, as a result, two families got to know each other better.

When we organize special events outside of the school day, we give our families additional opportunities to socialize and connect. At one YWCA center, assistant director Ms. Anne decided to plan a family night. Since in Minnesota winter weather is a prominent feature of daily life, she decided to celebrate the season with a winter-themed family night. She set up activities in the hallway, offering something for every age group, from infants to preschoolers.

Many children played at a sensory table with synthetic snow and scoops. Colorful markers frozen into ice cubes were a big hit too. The washable ink had colored the water as it froze, making a rainbow assortment of colorful ice cubes with markers for "handles." Children and families drew on a large sheet of paper hanging on the wall. It was a pastel and icy adventure. There were exciting aluminum foil–covered blocks to use for "ice" block building. Large plastic sensory bags filled with eye-catching colored water, oil, wintry snowflake charms, and glitter were taped down on trays for everyone to enjoy as they pressed and poked the bags to see what happened. Another big attraction was the winter dress-up area. Ms. Anne used a padded play ring from the gym to hold boots, snow pants, jackets, hats, mittens, and gloves. On the wall above, she made a poster with drawings of the clothing and the English, Spanish, and Somali words for them.

The families helped themselves to food and enjoyed eating their meals together. Staff from the center talked with families and made introductions when needed. As a result of this family night, new networks developed, and existing relationships grew stronger.

Teachers also have access to professional development networks that provide us with research and information about child development. A YWCA teacher found a creative way to share what she was learning with her families. Here is her story.

Ms. Dianne thought parents might like to learn about the benefits of play. She made a plan to engage with families and set the following goals: make it fun, make it accessible, and help parents extend classroom learning at home.

On Monday, the class made a large batch of play "snow." These were the ingredients:

- 2 parts baking soda
- 1 part baking powder
- 1 part liquid soap

Ms. Dianne let the children choose between a few essential oils and liquid watercolor paints to add to the recipe. The class decided to include blue paint and a pine scent. They gathered around the sensory table to measure, mix, play, and learn.

On Tuesday, they made another batch of snow. This time, they chose pink paint and lavender oil.

On Wednesday, Ms. Dianne and her group worked together to remember and record the steps for making snow. They also decorated construction paper with drawings and open-ended materials like tissue paper, glitter, ribbon, and yarn. During naptime, Ms. Dianne photocopied the directions. She also wrote a short paragraph explaining how engaging all five senses encourages brain development in children. In addition, she emphasized the importance of learning through play and provided tips on how to stay calm and positive during messy play. Ms. Dianne included a note at the bottom that said, "If you would like more information on the research about play, let me know and I'll get it to you."

On Thursday, Ms. Dianne asked the class to glue the directions for play snow to their construction paper drawings. She wrote, "Play is learning" on the back of their work.

On Friday, the students measured one-half cup of baking soda and one-quarter cup of baking powder into zip-top plastic bags. Ms. Dianne stapled on additional directions that read: "Play Snow. Add liquid dish soap a tablespoon at a time and mix. Keep adding soap until the snow is as sticky or dry as you like." She also included tips on possible additions like essential oils and paint. She was excited to share the lesson with parents, and her students were too.

## Goal three: Acknowledge and respect culture

A premise of anti-bias teaching is that interactions between all people matter. The interactions between adults, between teachers and children, and between children all create a culture. This phenomenon perpetuates itself: just as our interactions shape center culture, the center culture shapes our interactions.

At the YWCA, we work to create a culture of mutual respect and support. One teacher, Mr. Kai, used specific anti-bias strategies to honor a family's culture and to show that he was a trustworthy and sensitive teaching partner. Here is his story.

Javon's parents were worried. Their son spoke Spanish at home but would be expected to speak English at school. Would it be too challenging for him to learn and communicate with his peers? Javon's parents decided to share their concerns with his teacher, Mr. Kai.

Mr. Kai had connected with the family on other occasions—during conferences, pickup and drop-off times, and school events. He knew that, with the exception of Javon's grandmother, the family members spoke Spanish and English but spoke only Spanish at home.

At their meeting, Mr. Kai greeted Javon's parents with a smile. He welcomed them into the classroom with warm handshakes. After Mr. Kai made sure they were comfortable, he listened intently to their concerns. Mr. Kai was bilingual, so he had a personal framework to understand where Javon's parents were coming from. He also had the knowledge and expertise to explain the preschool dual-language learning process.

Since Mr. Kai and Javon's family had talked about their communication preferences at their initial conference, Mr. Kai knew their communication styles differed. He used a reflective listening strategy to make sure he was understanding the family's concerns.

"I hear you say you are worried about Javon learning to talk with his friends at school because you speak Spanish at home. Is that right?" he asked.

"Yes," they agreed.

Mr. Kai assured them that Javon was doing well in school and was confidently communicating in English with everyone in the classroom.

"Javon plays with two boys a lot right now. They have been building towers. Here is their work." He pointed to a tall structure that had a handwritten sign with the children's names and the words "work in progress." It was easy to distinguish Javon's handwriting on the sign.

Mr. Kai also shared more classroom activities and described Javon's learning experiences by showing his work portfolio. "We have been taking turns choosing songs for the group in circle time, and the students are getting the chance to pick out books to practice reading to their friends," Mr. Kai explained. "Javon loves to be the teacher and really has fun."

Mr. Kai and Javon's parents had a productive discussion on the benefits and challenges for Javon as a bilingual preschool student. They shared that they really wanted Javon to learn English, and Mr. Kai was able to show them evidence that Javon was learning English and more. Mr. Kai also wanted them to know that Javon was not the only student who spoke more than one language. He made sure to show Javon's parents the classroom word wall where the students' vocabulary words of the week were displayed in Spanish, Somali, and English. Mr. Kai asked if they would like more information about dual-language learning and shared some resources he had printed off in preparation for their conversation.

The meeting was a success. Javon's parents felt good about Javon being bilingual. They were happy he was in Mr. Kai's classroom. Mr. Kai appreciated the opportunity to get to know Javon and his family better. He knew that the more comfortable Javon's parents felt with him, the more comfortable Javon would feel as he continued to learn and grow.

## Goal four: Share information through two-way communication

From business development to early childhood education, there is a common understanding that communication is the key factor in turning relationships into partnerships. Leadership is closely linked to teaching.

Again, as we do not have the time or space to cover every aspect of how we find this concept relatable and important to anti-bias teacher and we invite you to access our provided additional resources. For this segment of our work, we can generalize concepts of leadership styles can be found in works such as *Leadership Theory and Practice* by Peter

Guy Northouse (2018), and specifically for the field of ECE, in *The Three Rs of Leadership: Building Effective Early Childhood Programs through Relationships, Reciprocal Learning, and Reflection* by Julie K. Biddle (2012) (see leadership styles in Peter Guy Northouse 2018 and specifically in early childhood in Biddle 2012). We think this principle means that two-way communication is the foundation of intentional, anti-bias family-teacher partnerships. Gregory Cheatham and Sylvia Nyegenye (2017) would agree, especially for culturally and linguistically different people, that "two-way dialogue necessitates both teachers and parents sharing and collaboratively characterizing young children's strengths and needs" (686). Communication is a tool that families and teachers use to share power and make decisions.

Even people from the same culture who speak the same language can have difficulties communicating. Communication between people who do not speak the same language introduces an additional challenge. At the YWCA, we use the following communication strategies:

## First Meetings

During our first meeting with families:

- We invite them to be part of their child's teaching team.
- We let them know that we value and welcome their questions.
- We assure them that all concerns are taken seriously.
- We find out how parents/caregivers like to communicate.
- We listen to their goals for their child.
- We give them information about our program, philosophy, and values.
- We introduce them to the other teachers and staff.

We know this initial conversation gives us information about the child, which will then guide our feedback and the way we deliver information to the family in the future. One YWCA teacher keeps a close eye on new families to make sure they settle into the center culture: "I like to spend extra time with new parents when they drop off or pick up their children," said Mr. Russell. "It's good to check in with them for questions or concerns. You want families to feel welcome and at home in their child's new learning environment."

## Everyday Communication

Every interaction we have with families sets the tone for our relationships with them. Families need to know that they are welcome every day, not just when they are new to our programs. Student drop-offs and pickups are excellent times to create a culture of high-quality communication. Teachers can

- say hello and goodbye;
- ask about family activities, plans, and events outside of the center;
- share a positive story or note about a student;
- show parents they are important by using their names; and
- talk about upcoming classroom activities.

Through this daily contact, teachers and families can build trust and develop sincere relationships. Daily contact is just one of many ways to connect to families. In fact, we have found that daily communication makes planned communication even better. When teachers plan with families for a call or face-to-face meeting, the outcomes are far more positive.

## *Planned Communication*

The first meeting with families sets the stage, and then daily, quick hellos and goodbyes can keep positive feelings flowing. There is also planned communication. Weekly or monthly newsletters and documentation boards of children's work can show families some highlights and the depth of learning their children are being exposed to on a daily basis. Setting a time for a phone call, private check-in, or specific meeting even if it is not conference time is an excellent way to strengthen the necessary bond between teachers and families. While it is easy and natural to use pickup and drop-off as the main time for communication, we want to emphasize that small doses of individual time is exceptional. We say "exceptional" because dedicating specific time to a conversation as opposed to a quick hello or impromptu but important chat is uncommon, not terribly difficult, and will likely help build powerful alliances between teachers and caregivers. Not only does it help families but it will also help the teacher and child. The flow of two-way communication can often be clearer when the teacher is not also trying to engage with the classroom while holding a quick and important chat with a family member who is on the way in or out the door.

## *Making Sure Your Meaning Is Understood*

Successful communication between families and teachers does not happen by accident. Teachers must clearly articulate their ideas and thoughts and use active listening techniques. Both written and oral communication must be open, welcoming, and respectful. Communicating in ways that respect and support families requires awareness of several different aspects of communication, including word choice, tone, language, and nonverbal communication through body language.

Our teachers view every message home as an opportunity to build stronger relationships. "I try to choose my words carefully," Ms. Dianne said. "It's hard to think about the message I am sending to families that is beyond just the words."

## Chapter Point Summary

1. Each family is unique.
2. Children build their self-identity though experiences over time with families and community, and these experiences also shape their development.
3. It is the teacher's responsibility to build relationships with families for the well-being of the child; teachers' interactions, especially with families, are a profound factor in children's growth and development.
4. There are four main goals we strive for when working with families:

   - Share power.
   - Build networks of support.
   - Respect culture.
   - Create avenues of two-way communication.

# CHAPTER FIVE
# Domains and Standards

*How can I use the domains and standards
to guide anti-bias teaching?*

The YWCA Minneapolis anti-bias curriculum uses research-based, nationally recognized standards to define teaching goals and guide practice. Each state has various ways of laying out the quality requirements for its youngest citizens. Nationwide, early learning program standards are not perfectly aligned, but they are generally reflective of each other. In 2002, the National Association for the Education of Young Children (NAEYC) and National Association of Early Childhood Specialists in State Departments of Education (NAECS/SDE) jointly adopted a position statement on early learning standards, which says that standards must be developmentally appropriate. We think the *way* we make standards developmentally appropriate is through understanding bias (chapter 2), teacher education—especially self-reflection (chapter 3), including children's families in their learning (chapter 4), and connecting to authentic observation (chapter 6). In this way, an anti-bias teacher can really make learning happen through play (chapter 7). When standards are correctly implemented, it enables teachers to

- mark the learning process and describe child behavior;
- champion children;
- watch for implicit and cognitive bias;
- connect behavior to child development;
- explain why and how play-based learning works; and
- set and support learning goals.

NAEYC and NAECS/SD (2002) take the position that meeting standards is the teachers' responsibility, rather than something children have to "do." We completely agree! Standards help teachers explore the strengths of every child, every day. This enables us to set developmentally appropriate learning expectations for our students.

Keeping these goals in mind, we can listen and look for the learning opportunities that will inspire each child to grow. This takes flexibility in planning and teaching. As anti-bias practitioners, we seek to understand and celebrate the individuality of each child. In addition, when we combine our individualized approach with clear learning domains and standards, we can lead—rather than follow—the development of children.

Standards help us design meaningful activities that

- encourage problem solving;
- inspire creativity;
- promote curiosity; and

- use student questions to drive learning.

It is imperative to remember that children are best able to reach these standards through play—that is when the magic happens! We talk more about that in chapter 7, but for now, let's look at how learning standards shape a solid anti-bias play-based learning environment.

## Credible Standards Challenge Biased Thinking

Learning domains and standards give us the objective information we need to question our assumptions, fine-tune our practice, and put children and families first. The more we understand our students' perspectives, the better we can be at helping them recognize and reject bias. Our guidance in unraveling bias matters.

In chapter 2 we explained that children make their own meaning about race and culture, with or without a teacher to support them. However, having a positive teaching presence makes all the difference. Teachers help make the connections to anti-bias thinking in the daily activities of a preschool classroom.

We think that everything, from washing hands to taking a walk, can playfully connect to domains and standards. The exciting thing is—they can also be supported by an anti-bias culture!

## Learning Domains

The YWCA anti-bias curriculum has seven learning domains:

1. Social and Emotional Development (SE)
2. Approaches to Learning (AL)
3. Language and Literacy (LL)
4. Creativity and the Arts (CA)
5. Mathematical Development (MD)
6. Scientific Thinking (ST)
7. Physical and Motor Development (PM)

These domains align with NAEYC's five general standards: social, emotional, physical, language, and cognitive. We have also drawn heavily from Minnesota's eight domains. You can view the Early Childhood Indicators of Progress: Minnesota's Early Learning webpage at https://education.mn.gov/MDE/dse/early/highqualel/ind.

We invite you to use the "State and National Alignment to YWCA Minneapolis Curricula: Domain Alignment" chart here to see how your state or your current curriculum domains align to the YWCA anti-bias curriculum.

| STATE AND NATIONAL ALIGNMENT TO YWCA MINNEAPOLIS CURRICULA: DOMAIN ALIGNMENT | | | |
|---|---|---|---|
| **YWCA Minneapolis** | **NAEYC** | **MN ECIPs (2020)** | **Your State or Curriculum** |
| Social and Emotional Development | Social Emotional | Social Emotional & Social Systems Cognitive | |
| Approaches to Learning | Cognitive | Approaches to Learning | |
| Language and Literacy | Language | Language, Literacy, Communications | |
| Creativity and the Arts | Cognitive | The Arts | |
| Mathematical Development | Cognitive | Mathematics | |
| Scientific Thinking | Cognitive | Scientific Thinking | |
| Physical and Motor Development | Physical | Physical and Movement | |

Within the YWCA domains are standards. We aligned our standards with Minnesota's components as well. You can use the worksheet "Domain and Standards Alignment" here to compare your state or preferred curriculum standards to ours.

| DOMAIN AND STANDARDS ALIGNMENT | | |
|---|---|---|
| **YWCA** | **MN Domain & Component** | **Your State/Curriculum** |
| I. Social and Emotional Development | | |
| SE1 Emotional Security | SE Component 4–5: Self-Management | |
| SE2 Self-Awareness | SE Component 1–3: Self and Emotional Awareness | |
| SE3 Community, People, and Relationships | SE Component 1–3: Self and Emotional Awareness & 6 – 8 Social Understanding and Relationships | |
| SE4 Change over Time | SS Component 3–4: Change Over Time | |

## DOMAIN AND STANDARDS ALIGNMENT

| YWCA | MN Domain & Component | Your State/Curriculum |
|---|---|---|
| SE5 Social Understandings and Relationships | SE Component 1–3: Self and Emotional Awareness | |
| II. Approaches to Learning | | |
| AL 1 Inventiveness, Problem Solving, and Curiosity | AL 1–2: Initiative and Curiosity | |
| AL 2 Interest and Persistence | AL 3–6: Attentiveness, Engagement, and Persistence | |
| AL 3 Processing and Utilizing Information | AL 7–9: Creativity & 10–13 Processing and Utilizing Information | |
| III. Language and Literacy | | |
| LL 1 Listening, Understanding, Communicating, and Speaking | LLC 1– 2: Listening and Understanding; Receptive Language & 3 – 4 Communicating and Speaking; Receptive Language | |
| LL 2 Emergent Reading Skills | LLC 5–13: Emergent Reading | |
| LL 3 Emergent Writing Skills | LLC 14: Writing | |
| LL 4 Computer Knowledge | SS 8: Technology | |
| IV. Creativity and the Arts | | |
| CA 1 Exploring and Expression | A 1-2 Exploring the Arts, 3-4: Using the Arts to Express Ideas and Emotions, & 5: Self Expression in the Arts | |
| CA 2 Music and Movement | The Arts 1–5 | |
| CA 3 Dramatic Play | Approaches to Learning 7–9, 11 | |
| V. Mathematical Development | | |
| MD 1 Numerals and Patterns | M 1-6: Number Knowledge & 7: Measurement | |
| MD 2 Measurement | M 7: Measurement & 8: Patterns | |
| MD 3 Geometry, Spatial Thinking, and Data Analysis | M 9–11: Geometry and Spatial Thinking, 12-13: Data Analysis | |
| VI. Scientific Thinking | | |
| ST 1 Discover, Act, and Apply Strategies | ST 1– 2: Discover & 3 – 4: Act | |
| VII. Physical and Motor Development | | |
| PM 1 Large Motor Skills | PM 1– 4: Gross Motor | |
| PM 2 Fine Motor Skills | PM 5– 6: Fine Motor | |
| PM 3 Healthy and Safe Living Practices | SS 1–2: Community, People, and Relationships & 5 – 6: Environment | |

## Domain One: Social and Emotional Development

In this curriculum, the domain of Social and Emotional Development has five standards:

1. Emotional Security
2. Self-Awareness
3. Community, People, and Relationships
4. Change Over Time
5. Social Understandings and Relationships

Social and emotional growth and development influence all other learning. Implementing intentional strategies to support skill development in this area will set our students up for greater success in the other domains. A secure child is able to take risks, learn, and grow. Beyond planned learning activities, teachers can also promote stability by creating predictable routines during daily activities, including the following:

- pickup
- drop-off
- mealtimes
- toileting
- transitions

Teachers help students feel safe by connecting with their families in a way that is culturally responsive and builds authentic relationships. That kind of development is supported in standard 3, Community, People, and Relationships.

As we read the social and emotional learning domain standards, we can reflect on things we already do and plan new opportunities that will support growth and development. We can also make sure we set developmentally appropriate behavioral expectations in our classrooms. It is important to notice what social and emotional proficiency looks like for each age group; a common error is to expect preschoolers to behave like kindergartners. Just as an infant should not be expected to act like a toddler and teenagers should not be expected to act like adults, we cannot set unrealistic expectations for our students.

Social and emotional standards can be especially helpful as we evaluate and address behaviors. There can be many reasons for behaviors, so it is important to evaluate your own bias before determining the cause and purpose of a behavior. Some common behaviors that require teacher intervention or attention include the following:

- **Regression:** A child is likely seeking emotional support. Often when children are acting younger or needier than their usual behavior, it is because they need reassurance. It is helpful to think of this as the child "going back" to the last level they felt the most cared for. For example, a preschool-age child might want a pacifier in the early stages of integrating a new baby into the family or during any other transition.

- **Using strategies that work in other environments:** A child may be struggling to differentiate between home and school rules. Children behave in ways that have worked for them. If reasoning with an adult at home to extend playtime before naptime is welcomed by the parent as an opportunity to build independence but in class teachers view this behavior as disruptive, insolent, or selfish, the child is being misunderstood. A teacher can look for the ways the child is modeling understanding of the primary environment and work to adjust expectations or set parameters ahead of potential conflicts.

- **Testing limits:** A child may be looking for consistent rules. Closely linked to using strategies that have worked in other environments, children look for consistency to feel safe. Sometimes the less safe children feel, the more they will test limits; conversely sometimes the safer children feel, the more empowered they feel to test limits. Understanding limit setting for individual children is closely tied to knowing their primary caregiver's style of behavior guidance.

- **Having a flight, fright, or freeze response:** This is oftentimes a stress response. If children are "freezers" they will withdraw when stressed. A teacher who is put off by this might insist that the children join the group anyway and "just get over it," but this will not address the underlying problem. Likewise, a child who becomes aggressive, cries, or tries to run is sometimes labeled as "out of control." Children typically will seek to self-soothe, so if they need to move to calm down, forcing them to sit is counterproductive. Try an impromptu jumping jack session to replace unsafe behaviors such as running away or hitting.

- **Destructive and disorganized behavior:** Children may be overstimulated or understimulated; they could also be struggling to manage their stress or physiological and emotional needs. Does the child need some sensory sand to squeeze? Is it time for a drink of water and a break?

In order to get an authentic picture of child development and promote healthy growth, teachers must put students' social and emotional needs first. We must build consistent routines with plenty of time for children to master their emotional and social intelligence, gain self-help skills, and solve problems.

Let us review the anti-bias learning goals developed by Louise Derman-Sparks and Julie Olsen Edwards (2020) to see how they can guide our work within the social and emotional domain.

1. Identity: Have increased self-awareness, confidence, family pride, and positive social identity.
2. Diversity: Express comfort and joy with human diversity, accurate language for human differences, and deep, caring human connections.
3. Justice: Increasingly recognize unfairness, have language to describe unfairness, and understand that unfairness hurts.
4. Activism: Demonstrate empowerment and the skills to act, with others or alone, against prejudice and/or discriminatory actions.

These anti-bias goals have an obvious connection to social and emotional learning standards, although these goals are obtainable in each and every domain because we don't limit our exploration and celebration of human differences to social and emotional learning. As we plan all activities, we must be on the lookout for opportunities to support equity and to honor our individual backgrounds.

In each domain there are categories that help us define when the standard is emerging, developing, or becoming proficient. It is important to note that proficiency in any category does not mean children will be perfect all the time, it means they will be successful often and with some support.

## Standard one: Emotional Security

With a teacher's guidance, children will learn to sustain their interest, name their feelings, handle limits, regulate behaviors, and express emotions in positive ways. They can also begin to build a positive self-image. Teachers can influence this by encouraging students to name their skills, talents, characteristics, and preferences. The "Windows and Doors" activity from chapter 3 can be modified for children to help strengthen their emotional security and sense of self. Or talk with children about what things they are expected to do at home, in school, or in their community. Make collages that show children doing their "work." Remember, all cultures have different expectations for children. Your group might talk about helping with dinner, dishes, and cleaning in the home. They might talk about playing with friends or family. Whatever the expectations, this activity can help children articulate the differences between adult roles and responsibilities and their own. We think defining adult and child roles can be comforting and affirm for children that they are being cared for by the adults in their world so they can do their own work, which is playing and learning.

A primary source of emotional strength is the sense that we belong to a group—children belong to a family, community, culture, and school program. We can affirm children's positive sense of self by helping them name the ways they belong. Through belonging, children also learn to cooperate, interact, and communicate with kindness and respect. They learn to form more and more positive peer relationships.

| STANDARD ONE: EMOTIONAL SECURITY | | | |
|---|---|---|---|
| **Skill** | **Emerging** | **Developing** | **Proficiency** |
| SE1.1 Emotional recognition: Connects feelings with descriptive emotion words. | The child has increased skill and ability to recognize and name own emotions and feelings. For example, "I am happy" or "I am angry." Might remember a transition is coming and prepare self for the change. | Begins to understand and respond to emotions of other children. States feelings. For example, might tell a friend, "Stop, I don't like that." Says things like, "It makes me mad/happy when . . ." | Comfortably shares ideas and opinions. For example, says, "I need this [object] for my [project]." Understands how to regulate strong feelings and helps/ empathizes with others. Shows and discusses a variety of emotions, thoughts, and reasons for behaviors: for example, "I am feeling [emotion] so I [action]." |
| SE1.2 Interest and choice: Makes choices and maintains focus in areas of interest. | Makes choices from a variety of options with support. Pays attention frequently to both familiar and new objects and experiences for longer periods of time. Stays with a wide variety of both adult and child- initiated activities. Shows a longer attention span and increased persistence in both child- and adult- directed activities. Might need help from an adult to clarify choices and guide the decision-making process. | Makes independent choices from a greater variety of options. In addition to exhibiting a longer attention span, self-directs within a greater variety of choices. May stop playing with initial choice and opt for another because the child "likes it." | Works at activity of choice for five or more minutes. Advocates for self-choices for play and learning. For example, may announce when coming in the room the intention to play with the blocks today. Or, if the block area is full, chooses dramatic play instead. |
| SE1.3 Emotional regulation: Enacts strategies for coping with emotions. | Accepts help and comfort or redirection when dealing with conflict. For example, accepts a hug when sad. | Handles strong emotions with strategies both new and practiced. Increasingly creates self-help situations. For example, might go to a "quiet/cozy corner" to "relax." More easily responds to adults' and friends' words and actions of comfort when facing difficulty. | Discusses alternatives to and solutions for problems. Talks through tasks, asking for adult assistance. Understands and operates within rules and structure. Stops and thinks before acting. May say, "I am taking big breaths because I am mad." |

| Skill | Emerging | Developing | Proficiency |
|---|---|---|---|
| SE1.4 Delayed Gratification: Uses self-help strategies for waiting. | With support can tolerate some waiting. May feel agitated or need comfort objects and actions. | With less support practices waiting. For example, says, "I can wait. I will get a drink of water." | Can comfortably wait or delay gratification. Child might say "just a minute" or "I need put the blocks away first." |

### Anti-Bias Learning Experiences

As a child's ability grows to confidently and effectively communicate their thoughts and responses instead of instinctively reacting in the midst of intense emotions, affirm their prosocial behaviors and those of others regularly. Mention those characteristics as a positive: "I love that you used your great big heart and beautiful [brown] hands to help your friends."

Make "Children's Jobs" collages. Especially when dealing with situations that are unstable or unpredictable, reminding children their job is to play, learn, and grow while grown-ups keep them safe can reduce potential emotional insecurities.

Provide learning experiences to construct and strengthen self-identity. For example, having intense emotions that make them feel bad does not make them a "bad" person.

Teachers can communicate ways they show love, patience, grace, and forgiveness. For example, help children articulate their foundation of love and support using pictures or other visuals to help them process this emotional language. Teachers can sing songs or recite rhymes or poems about people who love and are loved by each child.

## Standard two: Self-Awareness

An emerging sense of self shows up as a child's confidence to say what they want, what they like, and why they like it, as well as to make choices. For example, preschoolers may say that their favorite color is yellow and become angry when a classmate also chooses that as their favorite color. As children develop, and with the support of teachers, they will learn that others can share this preference. As they master their sense of self, they might also learn that they can have more than one favorite color or have certain colors they like for specific purposes.

When students try to accomplish their personal goals, they develop self-awareness. When a child says, "I did it!" or "I tried!" confidence grows. Anti-bias teachers are careful to place the spotlight on the process. We point out the enormous amount of effort it takes to try something. We see "failure" as an opportunity for growth.

Standards one and two provide developmental frameworks that tell us when and how to help our students build anti-bias perspectives. As we reinforce each student's self-awareness, confidence, and pride, we guide children toward reaching one of our anti-bias goals: developing a positive social identity.

| STANDARD TWO: SELF-AWARENES | | | |
|---|---|---|---|
| **Skill** | **Emerging** | **Developing** | **Proficiency** |
| SE2.1 Confidence and risk-taking: Demonstrates knowledge of environment and self through exploration | The child is beginning to self-describe personal interests and increasingly asks adults for help in getting needs that pertain to interests met. Child shows and talks about skills and abilities. For example, child might say, "I like dinosaurs" and ask an adult to play dinosaurs with her. Might try to open a door and wait for the opportunity to say he knows it is the teacher's job to touch doors in school. May say, "Look what I can do! Watch me!" | Practices real or play scenarios in which opportunities to demonstrate correct behavior or knowledge arise. For example, a child may pretend to fall and catch herself or deliberately make mistakes such as putting a spoon on his head. Might say, "I can try . . ." | More proficient in demonstrating acquired skills. Seeks feedback and opportunities for change. For example, a child is working in the sand table and asks for assistance from the teacher to build the tower higher. Might say, "I don't know how to do that yet." Takes on roles such as "teacher" in group time. Acknowledges accomplishments, saying, "I can hit the ball!" |
| SE2.2 Resiliency: Engages in mood recovery strategies | May cry, sulk, or despair when attempts to succeed in chosen endeavors are unsuccessful. Seeks and accepts comfort from others or favorite objects. | Seeks comfort frequently or in anticipation of difficulties with favorite objects, friends, or adults when upset. May choose a soft toy to hug as a way to say goodbye to a parent, for example. | Discusses abilities and opportunities for growth. May show recognition of self-comforting skills: "I used to cry when my mom left, now I hold my blanket. I am learning how to be okay." |
| SE2.3 Empathy: Demonstrates interest in and understanding of others' feelings | Begins to guess at what others might think or feel. Uses simple emotion words such as *happy* or *sad*. | Recognizes more complex emotions in others, such as lonely or excited. Begins to ask questions of others about their feelings. | Predicts others' emotions. For example, child says, "My mom will like my picture." Or, "I made this for you because you are sick and I want to make you happy." |
| SE2.4 Individual connection: Describes personal position in groups | Demonstrates awareness of self as part of a family, culture, community, or group. Might say, "We went to see [family or location]." | Greater awareness of details regarding self, family, or culture. Child might say, "My birthday is coming!" Can identify some aspects of family celebrations, traditions, and expectations. | Might describe details of a family event. For example, "I always do [this] for [event/holiday]." Details may or may not be correct, tries to describe details. |

| Skill | Emerging | Developing | Proficiency |
|---|---|---|---|
| SE2.5 Preference confidence: Exhibits understanding of personal likes and some willingness to accept others' choices. | Shares likes and dislikes in a confident manner. For example, may display some anger or challenge to others with different (dis)likes. | Shares likes and dislikes in a more confident manner. For example, may say, "That's my song," or "Blue is my favorite color." Allows for others' preferences. | Makes personal choices in play and expresses opinions. Child says, "I don't like strawberry. I like chocolate. Let's play we are making chocolate." |

**Anti-Bias Learning Experiences**

Encourage art projects such as skin tone paint mixing and magazine "like or dislike" collages.
  Make individuality charts, showcasing children's preferences in a colorful graph.
  Extend conversations about differences when they come up.
  Make family trees. Discuss family traditions, family structure possibilities, and ways families can be made.

## Standard three: Community, People, and Relationships

Teachers guide children as they learn that they belong to a group and they discover different types of groups. As they develop, children will notice and ask questions about people's physical, emotional, and personal similarities and differences. Respecting and acknowledging these differences in groups is a sign of social maturity.

Children might notice and describe the different roles they experience at home or at school. We might hear them say, "Today I am the table-setter. You are the dishwasher," or "Teacher, you open the door, right?" As children enter proficiency of this standard, they will expand their appreciation of social roles. They might say, "The officer directs traffic," or "Doctors help people who are hurt."

We can inspire children to develop in this area by giving them opportunities to work in a group and support others and their needs. We might encourage pretend play where children take orders for food, or we can ask the group members to share their ideas and make a graph of their findings. Children show competence by initiating games or songs. They may also point out rules of behavior and notice the different ways people celebrate holidays or traditions.

Some distinctions are easier to see and acknowledge. If a child said, "Only boys can be officers," an anti-bias teacher would notice there was some work to do around gender stereotypes. Other distinguishing comments are less easy for teachers to respond to. For example, some teachers have reported overhearing students saying things like "You are Black, and Black people are bad." Moments like these are very overt and important opportunities to correct racist statements. As we said previously, racism can make us all feel very uncomfortable, it hurts to hear words like this even from the youngest people. Teachers who have been in these situations agree that it was not a comfortable moment for them. Sometimes we also address moments like these after the fact by informing parents and center administrators, so they can work as a team to address misconceptions. It's important the teacher responds to the child in the moment: "I told her, 'Those words can hurt, and skin color does not make a person good or bad.' We talked to her parent and have kept working on it."

Addressing explicit racism is one way to work on building an anti-bias culture. Another way is through work that undermines racist and unfair concepts. For example, we can use puppets to play out an unfair situation, maybe like the one between the teacher and child above, and ask for the children to help resolve this together without putting a child in the blame spotlight.

As teachers, we can work to promote an appreciation of diversity. The American Psychological Association (2012) reminds us that diversity is not only about race, ethnicity, or sex, but these are often easier to identify. We should also build lessons toward a more complex understanding of individual differences to help children recognize the people and relationships in their community. As children move through this domain, we can encourage them to feel comfortable with diversity, teach them to use accurate language for human differences, and help them develop deep, caring human connections.

| STANDARD THREE: COMMUNITY, PEOPLE, AND RELATIONSHIPS | | | |
|---|---|---|---|
| **Skill** | **Emerging** | **Developing** | **Proficiency** |
| SE3.1 Group awareness: Describes group and individual differences. | The child begins to articulate separating others from self. For example, when another child is going home, the child may say, "I have to wait." | Talks about what people do at home or at work. May share what a family member does for work or fun. Begins to think about others' families and communities. Shares some stories about family and community. For example, may talk about a special meal or a party. May speak as though the child assumes you were at an event too. | Knows and describes child's role in the family and other groups. For example, may talk about things the child does to help the family. With greater accuracy can describe what "other" families and friends might do to celebrate or worship. May ask others what kind of party they had or what they did for a birthday, for example. |
| SE3.2 Group respect: Shows interest in the activities of others. | Considers individuality through questions and observations. Might ask, "What is [person] doing? Why?" | Begins to tell more accurate stories about family. For example, "At the park we . . ." Begins to notice others have families that have different experiences. | Affirms differences in others' families and other groups. For example, may say, "Some people take the bus, and some people drive a car." |

| Skill | Emerging | Developing | Proficiency |
|---|---|---|---|
| SE3.3 Group norms: Participates in group activities using expected behavior. | Participates in group activities with some assistance. For example, will clean up and join circle time with positive teacher support. May know there are class rules posted and still need help remembering to "use walking feet." | Follows expectations with greater fluidity. Might help others remember the rules and still need help herself. For example, child might remind another to "hold hands with a buddy" and still need reminders himself. May talk about others' roles, such as "She is the money-taker at the store." | Helps remind others of rules; shows increased behavior regulation. For example, may sit in circle time and announce she is waiting for the teacher if that is the expectation. May follow procedures with little help, such as hand washing after coughing. Participates in game development and can make some rules of play. For example, he will "stand and wait because I am the lookout" in an adventure game. |
| SE3.4 Group resolution: Participates in problem-solving activities. | Increasing willingness to solve issues, with adult or peer support as needed. May listen and yet not offer solutions to a group problem. | Increasingly recognizes the need for group decision-making. May attend a "family meeting" in play, for example. Acts in accordance with a group's plan for play or other activity. | Offers group solutions in play or other activities. Works to solve problems with increased regulation. Understands rules, reasons, and consequences. May say, "We can solve this." |
| SE3.5 Role maintenance: Maintains selected behavior for a purpose. | Can play a familiar role in a game such as a baby or a parent, pet, or child. Increased ability to sustain the role comes with practice. | Can switch or sustain roles in play as needed with some prompting. For example, may be willing to become the "customer" when needed. | Enjoys practicing and pretending to make decisions in play; may take polls/surveys/ask questions to decide who will be the "doctor" or the "teacher." |
| SE3.6 Group space awareness: Shows curiosity about familiar and novel environments. | Curious about places where people work, learn, live, and play. For example, gardens, sports, libraries, jobs, and vacations. May ask many questions about these and other locations. | With greater accuracy can describe some attributes of commonly visited or interesting new areas. For example, shares highlights of a novel experience such as a museum visit: "There was a big dinosaur." Or may be able to describe some details of the local playground or the home. | Uses words to describe physical features of a place. For example, "The building has pictures of kids on the wall" or "We walked up a great big hill." |

| Skill | Emerging | Developing | Proficiency |
|---|---|---|---|
| SE3.7 Resource awareness: Recognizes options for fulfilling needs with available resources. | Shows some interest in information about group needs, such as water, light, heat, or food. May ask or talk about these resources, for example, "I will buy food in the store." | Increasing awareness of how resources fulfill needs, such as birds bringing food to their babies or going shopping for food with a family member. May begin to discuss basic household needs like blankets, dish soap, and brooms/vacuums. | Uses available resources to solve a problem, such as getting tape or glue to fix a book. |
| SE3.8 Group member awareness: Recognizes groups are made of individuals. | Begins to understand that members of groups are not the same in all characteristics. For example, might feel frustrated that someone shares a favorite color or may be delighted that a classmate has the same shoes. | Becomes more proficient at noticing differences within group identities. For example, she may notice that her mom wears a hijab to the mosque but not to work. A child might become aware that skin tones vary among classmates. | Uses more complex descriptions of specific qualities of self and others. For example, she might begin to make accurate or inaccurate statements about why in-group differences exist. She might wonder if her aunt is too hot to wear her hijab to work, or he might ask why we all have different color hair, eyes or skin. |

### Anti-Bias Learning Experiences

Provide accurate information about why differences exist. Mix skin tone paint to explore the differences among classmates' self-portraits.

With children, make and decorate a Venn diagram of roles and responsibilities for community jobs, home jobs, or classroom jobs. Take pictures of children doing "jobs."

Ask for photos of family members at work or home doing specific tasks.

Use play experiences to encourage boys and girls to explore challenging gender stereotypes. For example, scientists, farmers, doctors, lawyers, bus drivers, teachers: who can do these jobs and why? Make a dress-up barber shop, salon, restaurant, pet groomer, doctor, police/fire station, grocery store, farm, or dentist. Emphasize equity for women and people of color. We can all be scholars, construction workers, teachers, parents, doctors, and so on.

Make maps with shapes, images, photos, paint, and other free-form materials. Go on scavenger hunts in the community or neighborhoods.

Make needs and wants collages.

## Standard four: Changes over Time

Teachers guide children toward learning that things change. Children who begin to understand past, present, and future are able to emotionally manage the ever-changing landscape of life. Emerging evidence of this standard may show up in language such as, "One time when I was little . . ." or "She is older than me" or "My mom is bigger than you." Children may seek to place value on where people are on the spectrum of interest. For example, do we overtly or inadvertently support attitudes that it is better to be bigger, older, faster, or stronger? What do messages like this send to young children who are working hard every day to grow? Teacher Anne said she dealt with the competitive nature of her class when it came to speed and strength by developing a "personal best" culture. If the children wanted to race, for example, she would count and write the time for each child. The next "race" would be against the self. She explained, "This was a way to show development, strength, perseverance, and interest over time and helped the children's spotlight to be on their own bodies rather than others around them."

As their understanding about the concept of change increases, so too will the child's ability to more accurately describe what has been, what is coming, or what will be. For example, children begin to recognize that there are chronological orders to people's ages. Children may start to describe how they felt during activities or events with family or friends. They may tell detailed stories.

When children are gaining proficiency in this standard, their ability to describe past events increases, as does their ability to anticipate what activity is coming next. It becomes increasingly important for the child to tell us what will happen to them and others, as well as why and how it will happen.

| STANDARD FOUR: CHANGES OVER TIME | | | |
|---|---|---|---|
| Skill | Emerging | Developing | Proficiency |
| SE4.1 Past, present, future: Demonstrates awareness of time. | The child may talk about tomorrow or yesterday with some accuracy. For example, may say, "A long, long time ago . . ." or "Yesterday we played . . ." | Uses language to describe past or present events with increased accuracy and varied words. For example, "When I was little" or "We did that last time." | Using more complex time descriptors. For example, "First we did [this], and then we did [that]" or "When I get bigger I will . . ." |
| SE4.2 Memory interaction: Uses past experiences to inform current behavior. | Remembers past events and experiences with some help/guidance from others. For example, can "play" zookeeper when remembering the past field trip. | With some assistance he can demonstrate awareness of "What could happen if . . ." or "What happened last time?" With some collaboration and support she tries to remember where she was in the game to pick up where she left off the previous day. | With less assistance can remember past experiences. May remind the teacher that they were going to play puzzles after nap, for example. Needs less help remembering where the game left off; for example, if the zookeeper was checking on the animals, the child might choose to begin the game there. |

| Skill | Emerging | Developing | Proficiency |
|---|---|---|---|
| SE4.3 Routine awareness: Expresses comfort or interest in new and familiar activities. | Demonstrates comfort with routine tasks. Begins to comment on schedule or routine change. Might begin to remember the chronology of daily activities with greater accuracy. May say, "I know" when reminded that it is almost time to transition to a new activity during the day. | Can help make plans for events and sequences. For example, can help make plans to get ready for a new activity. Will be the "bell ringer" to signal the end of playtime. | Shows an increased awareness of scheduling and pending events. May say, "It's almost time to go home" and begin to clean up. |

### Anti-Bias Learning Experiences

Ask children to tell you a story, real or fictional. Write their stories down, making sure to use concepts like first, second, last or beginning, middle, and end. Affirm the individuality of choices and preferences in the child's storytelling. For example, if the story being shared is about making latkes and another child says, "Yuck, what's that?" a teacher can affirm the food preference and encourage understanding. Similarly, if all members of a group of children like pancakes, consider making a pancake diversity book or chart. There are many pancake-like foods around the world and in nearly every culture. This activity reinforces step-by-step planning while also broadening awareness of cultural and individual differences, even in a homogenous group.

Collect family stories using past, present, and future concepts.

Ask families for photos of events, their neighborhood street, homes, and so on. Use clean recyclable food (cereal, milk, rice and so on) or personal care (shampoo, hair oil) containers from children's homes in the dramatic play areas.

Have families bring in baby pictures to put with the children's school picture—discuss how children have grown. Teachers can emphasize how all children have grown and point out specific ways each child has changed.

Please note: This activity should be done carefully. Teachers must be sensitive to diversity of families. For example, are there children who are in foster care, adopted, in single parent homes, or have close family members estranged or gone for any reason?

## Standard five: Social Understandings and Relationships

Teachers guide children in learning to build friendships and have positive interactions with others. Children will begin to notice and be concerned for others' welfare. They become more skilled in understanding separations. They can find comfort with the people they like and trust. We think trusting and liking a person is a complex process, and it can be reinforced through consistent teacher-supported behaviors. During a professional development session, Ms. Anne explained that her center did not have racial or ethnic diversity and wondered how she could or if she should try to teach about diverse people. We say yes! After supported conversation, the teacher began to look in her community to find groups that could offer her class interesting and new perspectives. She found an elder community and built a story-sharing time between children and community elders. An ensuing trip to the library also yielded books about Native Peoples and a variety of cultures in her community that had previously been unnoticed. Anne reported that she was in the process of planning a year of opportunities woven into her existing curricula.

Anne told us that when she first took her group to the elder living center, Justice hung back by her side as the elders and children were introduced. Grandma Jean, as she asked to be called, sat in a chair smiling at the children. Anne pointed out that she had a blue shirt just like Justice. With some gentle encouragement, Grandma Jean and Justice then noticed they both had Js for their name and were soon reading the story Justice had chosen to share for the day.

As their skills develop, children have greater compassion for the feelings of others, and they can label emotions. They might also make predictions about how and why a person is feeling a particular emotion. They feel confident and will often expect to be welcomed into play.

As we move students toward the anti-bias goals of justice and activism, this domain can help us fine-tune our teaching so that we can be sure we introduce these concepts in developmentally appropriate ways. As children become more skilled in social and emotional standards, they will have a stronger ability to offer comfort, create solutions, and share perspectives. Masters of this standard may ask others how they are feeling and share their own perspective as a way to develop stronger alliances through shared points of view.

| STANDARD FIVE: SOCIAL UNDERSTANDINGS AND RELATIONSHIPS | | | |
| --- | --- | --- | --- |
| **Skill** | **Emerging** | **Developing** | **Proficiency** |
| SE5.1 Social diversity: Demonstrates interest and curiosity in both novel and familiar environments. | The child shows awareness of self as a part of a group or family. May talk about friends and people in his home. May use words that describe race, religion, or ethnicities in such a way that shows she thinks all people share the same experience. For example, a child might make a statement heard at her mosque or church in conversation. | May discuss some family concepts. For example, may say "in our house we celebrate Eid." Describes race, religion, or ethnicity in such a way that shows an awareness of separate groups. For example, he might ask a child what her church is called. She might ask why people have different skin tones or wear particular pieces of clothing. | May talk about ways other families celebrate special events. Children in this stage may begin to show deeper awareness of distinct social groups or races. For example, she might say, "There are many kinds of Black people. Some have different skin colors and live all over the world." |

| Skill | Emerging | Developing | Proficiency |
|---|---|---|---|
| SE5.2 Gender expression and identity: Uses gender terms to describe self or others— need not be conforming. | May describe self or others as a boy or girl with different levels of fluidity. May say "I'm a big boy/girl!" or "I am her daughter/son." | With greater ease can describe differences noticed among genders and with varying levels of accuracy. Might say, "Moms can only do [that]" or might ask, "Can boys can wear dresses too?" or "Girls can play basketball, right?" | With more accuracy describes a variety of skills men, women, boys, and girls may have. Might say, "He is a nurse, she is the construction worker." Is more skilled at naming ways a variety of women and men may exist in their world. |
| SE5.3 Gender identity: Demonstrates awareness of the association between physical and psychological gender identities | Shows increasing sex and gender awareness. Might say, "I am a girl" or may make statements such as "Girls can sit when they go to the bathroom and boys can stand." Gender roles maybe fluid; for example, a girl might say she is a boy and use the toilet standing up. | Greater sex and gender awareness. Children may use terms such as "boy" or "girl" and they can apply them as they choose. Might say "Boys and girls can be doctors." Children may identify not as their assigned sex, and their use of pronouns can change frequently. | Shows greater awareness of personal gender differences and recognizes that a category does not necessarily apply the same for every individual. For example, might say, "My dad likes to wear pink, so it's not just for girls." |
| SE5.4 Distance awareness: Shows interest in time and space as it relates to personal security. | Shows interest and awareness of time and space. May use words to represent cities, states, and countries but with minimal understanding, such as, "My grandma lives far away in Nigeria. It's a long time to get there." | May share some personal awareness of social locations like churches, mosques, or other culturally specific places. May say, "We went to the Chinese market for our favorite noodles" or describe traveling long or short distances to specific locations. | Begins to understand locations have specific places in relationship to self. For example, might use blocks to identify own home and someone else's home. |

### Anti-Bias Learning Experiences

Make emotion charts for your classroom and ask children to describe their moods. Emotion charts can have space for children to put their name and/or photo under several emotions at once. For example, children may be "happy" to be with friends while being "sad" because they miss their parent. Encourage children to move their names/faces to different emotional categories as they change how they think and feel during the day.

Use gender fluidly: make charts, collages, images, or graphs to consider all of the ways that people of any gender can express themselves. For example, women can be ministers in a church, doctors, pilots, farmers. Men can be teachers, nurses, gardeners, and so on. Men or women can wear dresses, makeup, or long or short hair. Remember that talking about sexuality and gender are two separate concepts. We have used the Genderbread Person as a reference for teachers to bolster their understanding of these ideas. See www .genderbread.org for more information.

Make global maps of the near and far past as applicable to your individual classroom. Chart family and people in the neighborhood. Get creative—you can make photo trees or use recycled boxes to make three-dimensional network representations. Can you build a cardboard house that shows families and neighborhoods? Relating it to family may trigger some children who may not know their family's history or who may be displaced, so proceed with sensitivity. It could also cause children to repeat adult sentiments they are parroting. Extra care is needed with this exercise.

# Domain Two: Approaches to Learning

This domain considers the ways that children express an interest in their world. As anti-bias instructors, we must first establish our own self-reflective practice so we can create psychologically supportive and safe environments that support children's curiosity. From this starting point, we can guide children toward our anti-bias learning goals. This area in particular allows us to focus on encouraging curiosity and considering other points of view. We can guide each student to develop an internal sense of justice. They will be ready and able to solve problems and reject unfairness. They will become persistent partners in building more equitable environments, both inside and outside the classroom. It is very important to remember that this domain does not have a K-12 alignment. This means it is foundational to future learning skills in older children. Ways teachers support a child's approaches to learning can fuel a zest for life that carries them all the way through high school graduation!

This domain has three standards:

1. Inventiveness, Problem-Solving, and Curiosity
2. Interest and Persistence
3. Processing and Utilizing Information

We can support growth in this domain when we allow children to experiment without fear of making mistakes. Mistakes in learning are truly learning opportunities. The Approaches to Learning domain encourages "maybes," "what-ifs," and "could-bes." Anti-bias work also specifically supports trying new strategies to create better outcomes.

# Standard one: Inventiveness, Problem Solving, and Curiosity

Teachers guide children to develop creative-thinking skills and discover new ways of knowing. Preschoolers often want to know why. Sometimes we hear this question so much that it can be exhausting! It is important to remember that this marks a stage of learning and growth. When children want to know how and why things happen, they are showing development in inventive thinking.

Growth indicators include the following:

- using past experiences or bright ideas to solve problems
- discussing their thoughts and experiences
- showing greater independence in seeking answers
- finding more creative ways to play
- inventing
- finding uses for objects

Ms. Melina reported to us in a professional development session that Angel was always waking up early during naptime. He would yell for his friend to wake up too, and it was very frustrating for her. As part of a reflective practice, Ms. Melina looked at what her goals were for Angel. "I want him to get enough rest and not wake up the others," she said. Angel was used to being told to be quiet after nap and also used to pushing back against this request. As an alternative strategy, Melina decided to bring the issue up to the class in morning circle using puppets. "How can we help Puppy wake up and let her friends rest?" she asked the group. The class had many solutions to offer. "Go to the bathroom quietly!" said one, "Get a drink of water," offered another. "Play a puzzle," said a third. One child raised her hand and asked if it would be okay for Puppy to eat a small snack. This surprised Melina. Snack was not served until 3:30, but she wondered if Angel was hungry or wanted to play. Considering the ways Angel might be trying to fuel his interest in his environment led Ms. Melina to try a variety of ways to engage Angel appropriately when he woke up from nap before his classmates.

| STANDARD 1: INVENTIVENESS, PROBLEM SOLVING, AND CURIOSITY | | | |
|---|---|---|---|
| **Skill** | **Emerging** | **Developing** | **Proficiency** |
| AL1.1 Novelty awareness: Shows interest in novel experiences. | The child is eager to learn new things. For example, may become excited to learn there are new materials in the science center. Talks about something "new" such as experiences or a toy. | Increasingly uses materials in new ways. For example, tries to use feathers for painting. Becomes proactive with new ideas. May try bringing blocks to the playdough table or dress-up to the trucks. With curiosity, asks many questions about ways, means, and opportunities to try ideas. | Looks ahead for opportunities. For example, might look quickly around the classroom or new area to find something interesting. |

| Skill | Emerging | Developing | Proficiency |
|-------|----------|------------|-------------|
| AL1.2 Novelty engagement: Participates in novel experiences. | Begins deeper interactions with novel experiences. She may enjoy taking things apart to see how they work or are built. For example, rather than turning the hands, he might explore the inside of a clock to see the gears. | Engages with new experiences with greater confidence. For example, willingly explores a firefighter's boots during a classroom visit or attempts to manipulate a novel instrument even though "I don't know how to play it." | Comfortably chooses activities, especially made-up and new experiences. Is increasingly willing to invent roles or actions that are unknown. For example, as a space explorer, the child might use pretend technical language. |
| AL1.3 Alternatives: Seeks understanding and explanation of phenomena. | Asks lots of "how," "why," and "what if" questions. Child may ask, "How did you make the playdough?" | Tries alternative ways of putting materials together. For example, might tear paper and mix with water to make "playdough." | Willingly shares many ideas about how to use new items or materials. Child may think of new uses for playdough, such as wondering if playdough could be made into a real plate. |
| AL1.4 Problem resolution: Tries or offers solutions to problems. | Questions outcomes. For example, may wonder how sand fills a cup differently when there is water mixed in or not. | Creates problems in play. For example, "There is a fire" or "That is lava." Thinks of ways to use toys and materials to represent conditions; for example, the box is a car. | Child tries out role-playing with make-believe objects to "test" limits. For example, will pretend to break rules or play games where there is a "good" or "bad" person. Pretends a truck has a flat tire and there are no tools or acts out an emergency complicating the situation. |

**Anti-Bias Learning Experiences**

Foster children's natural curiosity and encourage them to try new experiences using their senses. When children try new experiences, they become aware of similarities and differences.

For example, suggest a moon exploration. Make a chart of children's varied ideas of what they would need to explore the moon. Help children learn to become aware of other's thoughts and different ideas. Make "moon" experiences together. Make "moon rocks" from blocks wrapped with tinfoil, create "moon carts" with recycled materials, make "space packs" with empty plastic bottles, straps, and tissue paper "fire." Explore what is different about the moon from where we live on the earth; for example, you might talk about and explore temperature, water, and soil.

In general, consider this domain as a reminder to ask "why," "what," and "how" questions. If someone says they like dogs, for example, make a game of being dogs or other favorite animals, pick any color, create a special howl . . . the possibilities are endless.

Create surprises in your room. If you hear children talking about an upcoming event, like a sports game, a doctor visit, or a birthday party, find items that connect to that experience. Bring these items in to your room and "hide" them where children will find them. Then watch and wait for your chance to help ignite their imaginations with new games and play experiences to deepen their experience and imagination related to the subject. For example, hide a toy Ferris wheel or a photo in a "surprise bag." Ask your group questions to help them guess what is in the bag. Whether they guess the item or not, when you bring out the item you will springboard your class discovery on the subject of fairs or amusement parks.

## Standard two: Interest and Persistence

Teachers must encourage children to stick with it when something is important to them. Approaches to Learning can be supported in any activity. Have you seen children who are willing to keep trying to do a task despite repeated interruptions or problems? They are displaying proficiency in this area.

The block area is one place we can easily spot growth in this standard. When children are building and some pieces are knocked down, we know they are able to maintain interest and persist when they repeatedly return fallen blocks to their places. Progress is also shown when they leave to go to the bathroom, return, and pick up where they left off.

Be aware of children's developmental understanding of needs versus wants and equality versus equity. An example we have seen used shows a photo of three children of different heights trying to see over the fence. If in fairness, the same size box is given to all the tall child is too high and the smallest child still cannot see. In equity, each child gets what they need to see over the fence. The small child's box may be taller than the child in the middle but this does not diminish anyone is anyway. Giving people what they need to be successful is the purpose of equity. Point out real-life examples as they occur so children can relate. Returning to the blocks example, if one child is okay with tearing down the structure, and another child wants or needs to save a different structure, that is okay and honored. Or, if one child cannot eat certain foods that another student enjoys, both are acceptable and respected. Being responsive in this way is an opportunity to show equity and respect and advance anti-bias learning goals. Offer children opportunities to discover the possible outcomes of a situation and its alternatives. This will teach them how to make choices based on new ideas and critical thinking.

Each child's tolerance for interruption and ability to persist will be different. At the YWCA, we believe children should have extended periods of play. It takes time to plan, play, and create roles and routines in play. With time to really focus on play, children can develop an ability to maintain interest. When planning and designing learning experiences, consider learning styles: hands-on, auditory, and visual.

| STANDARD TWO: INTEREST AND PERSISTENCE | | | |
|---|---|---|---|
| **Skill** | **Emerging** | **Developing** | **Proficiency** |
| AL2.1 Focus: Stays with activities for longer periods of time. | The child stays focused on activities of choice for longer time periods. For example, rather than two or three activities in choice time, the child is now becoming more engrossed in one. | Returns to activities after interruption with some adult assistance to reenter play. For example, with some help may remember what she was playing yesterday and pick up where she more or less left off. He is less distracted by what is going on around him when focused. | Develops intentional focus. For example, when asked what the child will play today, responds, "I played puzzles with Mom last night. I'm going to do more puzzles. I'm really good at puzzles." |
| AL2.2 Attention: Observes the behavior of others or phenomena. | Pays some attention to activities, such as watching what another is doing. Depending on interest level, may watch up to a minute per year of age. | Shows increased attention span. For example, may ask for a second story but tires of it midway through. | Attention span continues to increase. He may stay with a favorite activity for longer periods of time. She may become engrossed in activities to the point where she forgets she needs to use the bathroom. |
| AL2.3 Force of will: Demonstrates effort to stay with tasks or plans. | May start a task or activity and not finish it. For example, he may have a short burst of play with friends followed by another short period of alone time in the book area. | Engages in longer play with others. For example, in the dramatic play area, children pretend to be a family saying goodbye in the morning, going to work and school, and coming home. May bring the game up throughout the day. | Makes plans and follows through. For example, the child wants her uncle to see her work at school, so she talks to teachers and parents, invites the uncle, makes plans for the visit, and follows them. |
| AL2.4 Effort awareness: Exhibits awareness of physical or mental effort to achieve goals. | Becoming more aware of the benefit of the concept of effort. For example, may say, "Whew! This is hard work. I will keep trying" while pretending to load big, heavy boxes or blast into space. | Manages change or setbacks and persists. For example, pretends, "The machine broke and we need to fix it. Hurry!" Or in daily life, "Teachers work hard. I can give you a hug to help you keep trying." | Looks for opportunity in challenging situations and is positive and adaptable. For example, repeatedly attempts to tape two paper towel tubes together. |

When planning and designing learning experiences, consider learning styles: hands-on, auditory, and visual. Make sure that the activities show some diversity in characters and environments, allowing children to see diversity in all that they explore.

Understand that demonstrations of interest and persistence will look different in each child. Offer children learning experiences to discover the possibilities of a situation, look into alternatives, and make choices based on their new ideas and critical thinking. Each child's tolerance for interruption and ability to persist will be different.

Intentionally teach the difference between equality and equity. For example, make a song or chant about "I'm big and strong, and I won't give up." Then, talk about ways each child is bigger and stronger than they were last week or even earlier in the day. Give examples of how one child's demonstration of strength looks different from another's, and discuss how each child needs individual support to succeed. For example, when setting up for nap, some children might be able to carry one end of the cot alone but another child might need an adult or a second child to assist. Helping children just to the point where they need assistance is equity. Being explicit about this kind of differentiation can help support persistence in tasks of all varieties.

## Standard three: Processing and Utilizing Information

Teachers guide children to follow directions, schedules, and sequences. Dramatic play gives children many opportunities to practice these skills, and it can happen in all learning areas. For example, children might show growth when they load blocks in a cart, dump them, and then go back for a refill as part of a construction play scenario. Children try out what they have seen in their daily lives in the dramatic play areas. Dramatic play is an excellent area to offer guidance to let children try new roles, ask deep questions, and open up thinking to multiple perspectives.

As children progress through this standard, they start to think ahead, problem solve, and try to learn to do new and more difficult tasks. Children who gain proficiency in this domain acquire a greater capacity for remembering and following schedules. They can recall events and create story lines.

| STANDARD THREE: PROCESSING AND UTILIZING INFORMATION | | | |
|---|---|---|---|
| **Skill** | **Emerging** | **Developing** | **Proficiency** |
| AL3.1 Task ordering: Develops or follows processes | With some help the child remembers and follows multistep directions. For example, if he is asked to carry a box and place it on the table next to the door, he might need a reminder to "turn around" to see the table. | The child strives to manage directions that are more complex. Remembers and follows three- to four-step directions. For example, she may rush to the vehicle shed to get her favorite bike. When the teacher asks, "How do we wait?" the child might respond by standing on the curb rather than directly in front of the door. | More independently follows the daily schedule in class. May assist others by asking questions such as "Did you wash your hands?" or "Next we go outside, right?" |

| Skill | Emerging | Developing | Proficiency |
|---|---|---|---|
| AL2.2 Attention: AL3.2 Information structuring: Recognizes actions have consequences. | Uses thoughts or actions to support tasks. For example, a child might sing a song or poem like "This is the way we wash our hands" while washing toys. | Externalization of informational structures may become more apparent. A child might talk, hum, or gesture as she enacts tasks or plays either alone or with a group. For example, while washing toy animals she may say, "I'll be careful to keep the soap out of your eyes." | Is deliberate about the use of structures to support learning and play. For example, he might suggest, "We clap three times when it is the next person's turn" to help the group play hopscotch. |
| AL3.3 Humor concept correlation: Expresses interest and enjoyment in novel concept correlation. | Child begins to add jokes and humor to conversation or play. Begins to role-play in games. May be limited to a few jokes/roles. | Begins to create more stories, jokes, and pretend roles in conversation and play for the effect of humor and fun. May repeat for fun/learning/satisfaction. | May explain and help peers learn roles, songs, or jokes. May make jokes or songs with others and practice and repeat them for learning and enjoyment. |
| AL3.4 Symbolic play: Demonstrates ability to replace or substitute objects and ideas with real or imagined props. | Makes representations in play/learning. For example, with some guidance can pretend "this [chair] is the bus." | Uses more detailed symbolic actions and props in play. Begins to invent more and requires less adult guidance. | Incorporates many materials, including props, blocks, dramatic play, or written words into play/learning. |
| AL3.5 Strategic thinking: Practices prediction of cause and effect. | Asks for help in solving problems and discovery. Makes suggestions with a variety of reasons/outcomes. For example, with some guidance thinks of two or more ideas/solutions. | Makes predictions and hypothesizes. Tries to solve problems alone or in groups. Tries again when attempts to solve issues do not give the preferred result. | Is willing to include others' ideas in developing plans for play and discovery. Solves problems alone and in groups. Predicts outcomes and revises plans. |

### Anti-Bias Learning Experiences

Support children's interest and persistence in the topics of interest to them.

Support activism; focus on solving problems that relate to shifting power and supporting others. For example, think about cost, quality, access, and accessibility.

Make sure that the activities show diversity in characters, materials, and environments, allowing children to see diversity in all areas they explore.

Create task-orienting photo sequences or posters with the children represented in the classroom (handwashing photographs of the children actually doing the process) and symbolic representations of handmade play objects such as rain sticks, homemade drums, child-safe beanbags, baby quilts, blanket forts, and so on. Use idea or choice charts with photographic representations of objects or play centers that children could use to make decisions/solve problems. Consider first/then options and solution boxes.

Record children's thinking processes: in group conversations try writing down as many ideas children can think of that pertain to any subject of their choosing.

## Domain Three: Language and Literacy

The domain of language and literacy, as the name suggests, focuses on all aspects of communicating. Its standards include the following:

1. Listening, Understanding, Communicating, and Speaking
2. Emergent Reading Skills
3. Emergent Writing Skills
4. Computer Knowledge

To guide students toward proficiency we must understand that language acquisition is a complex process that requires skills like listening, paying attention, and processing information.

Earlier, we discussed the impact communication styles can have on our ability to form deep, trusting relationships with the people around us. When we support language and literacy development in our classroom, we work toward our anti-bias learning goals. Confident, sensitive communicators can listen to and comprehend diverse voices, work for justice, and speak out against prejudice and discrimination.

## Standard one: Listening, Understanding, Communicating, and Speaking

Teachers guide children toward responding to direct questions and following simple directions. Young children may use gestures and some symbolic language to show preferences and thoughts when this standard is emerging. If a child's home language is different from the one spoken within the care and education setting, teachers may need to use images, gestures, and sign language to support communication.

When understanding grows, so too does correct use of language. Words like "in" and "out," or "over," "beside," and "under" may begin to emerge. When children are responding correctly to oral directions, such as "Put the block on the table, put your paper in the cubby, and then line up to go outside," they are reaching proficiency in this standard. Engaging in conversations with more complex words and thoughts also shows approaching mastery of this standard.

We have seen that sometimes a teacher's methods of communicating are very different from what children are used to from other teachers and from their families. For

example, someone might say, "You are too soft with them; you need to be firm." Or, "You are too loud; you are scaring the children." We wonder what happens to children as they learn to navigate the different codes in which teachers speak. What happens if one consciously or unconsciously privileges one way of responding to spoken words over another? In a professional development session focused on communication, one teacher told us that she is very deliberate about teaching Black children the words she expects them to hear in kindergarten

because, she says, "That is not the way they are talked to at home. I'm from this community. I know how parents talk to their children, and it is not what they will hear in school."

This area is ripe for deep exploration. We will share some of our thinking with the caveat that this subject is varied, deep, and layered. Racism and cultural expectations play a large role in the ways we expect people to respond to communication. We cannot talk about language development without also seeking to explore the complexities that people of color or non-English speakers are facing even as they are very young children. Low income and non-white students in elementary and higher grades can experience distress when school and home cultures clash, manifesting in poor educational outcomes and high dropout rates (Cholewa and West-Olatunji 2008; Taggart 2017). Our formal educational systems for elementary and older grades are Eurocentric: teachers are taught how to engage in a world of academia and teach children to do the same. Ms. Kenya put it this way: "At home I tell my child to 'get that and bring it here,' but a teacher in the public school might say, 'Shanti, please retrieve the clipboard and put it on top of the shelf.'" The tone teacher Kenya used in each directive was different. Sometimes this is called *code switching* or a *colloquialism*. Ms. Kenya said that the schools her preschool students will soon attend are filled with teachers who use words the children don't hear at home. "I expose my preschoolers to words that they will hear. I know that a child will react to unfamiliar settings, and that includes language, tone, and behaviors in a variety of ways. If the teacher is even unconsciously biased against Black children for example, what if she thinks this child is being disobedient when she doesn't jump right to and do what is asked?" Students who speak African American Vernacular English are often negatively characterized by teachers, and research shows that children benefit from learning how to code switch from educated teachers (Thibodeaux et al. 2020). We do not think it fair or just that a child would be intentionally or unintentionally penalized for having different mannerisms or vocabulary than her teacher—but we know that they are, and there are decades of research to back it up. As another teacher added, speaking from her personal experience, "If they don't talk right, they could end up in jail or worse."

For all stages of this standard, teachers should keep in mind that communication styles are diverse. For example, all homes have their own communication environment, and within the home each person has a communication style. The ways in which children are familiar with listening and responding to adults in their lives will determine how they show up in class. If teachers are intentional about using repeated and different modes of communication with children, they can avoid inaccurate assumptions about a child's communication skills. A child called Reina had a disrupted relationship with her primary caregiver. She was not a strong communicator of her likes and dislikes. In fact, often when she was asked to share her thoughts or feelings, her eyes would fill with tears and she would steadfastly look down at her hands. Reina needed a way to communicate that was not verbal to show she was listening and understanding if not speaking very much yet. Through the support of family, specialists, and teachers, Reina used a thumbs-up, -down, or to the side to show if she was feeling good, bad, or somewhere in the middle. The symbols took the place of words and worked as a good strategy for this child as she was gaining other skills to help her participate more fully in her environment.

| STANDARD ONE: LISTENING, UNDERSTANDING, COMMUNICATING, AND SPEAKING | | | |
|---|---|---|---|
| **Skill** | **Emerging** | **Developing** | **Proficiency** |
| LL1.1 Responsiveness: Uses effort to participate in processes of interest. | With some guidance, the child pays closer attention to adult-given directions. May or may not look directly at speaker, will act on words said/heard but not immediately. | Responds to directions more in real time with less of a lag. May say directions with the speaker, may begin moving to comply before directions are done being given. | Child responds correctly or helps others with given directions. With greater ease can follow and anticipate strings of steps like "Put the blocks away, use the bathroom, get a drink of water, and line up to go outside." |
| LL1.2 Communicating: Is responsive in words or actions to environment and stimuli. | Verbally or nonverbally responds to speaker, including watching or moving when someone is speaking. Is able to follow "Put your finger on your nose if you can hear me." | Offers ideas more readily. For example, will try different words or gestures to show meaning and clarify wants or needs. For example, a child might stand next to a drinking fountain and say, "agua, hot." | Frequently shares ideas. May share some dual-language knowledge with support or independently. For example, may call out directions in a game of Simon Says or use two languages plus actions to show meaning. |

| Skill | Emerging | Developing | Proficiency |
|---|---|---|---|
| LL1.3 Sharing meaning: Participates in patterns of conversation. | May point or look to blocks when asked, "Where would you like to play?" or lead an adult to the bookshelf and point to a book. | Begins to have increased fluidity when answering questions. For example, when asked what she would like to do next, may say, "I want to paint." | Follows rules of discussion and basic directions. Has multiple (five or more) exchanges in conversation. |
| LL1.4 Concept building: Adds novel or familiar concepts to communication. | Responds with actions in conversations. For example, a teacher describes feeling excited and a child smiles and stands tall. | Makes logical connections. Responds to what one says with a related statement. Shares more information about situations and experiences. Offers ideas and thoughts in conversation and asks some questions. For example, in response to a teacher saying she was excited, the child will add comments about something that makes him excited too. | Asks questions to get help and more information and makes decisions based on information. Can give much more detail when prompted about specific events and situations. For example, will add more context to "What makes you excited?" when prompted in conversation. |
| LL1.5 Vocabulary: Increases use of novel and complex words. | Asks about unfamiliar words, shows interest in vocabulary words. For example, repeats the word "responsibility" when choosing class jobs. | Practices using new words. For example, asks, "Is that my possibility [responsibility]?" Words are not necessarily used or spoken accurately. Is persistent in using and speaking new words. | With greater accuracy uses new and more complex words in daily conversation with peers and adults. Can discern some meaning of new words or tries to guess at meaning in the context of sentence. |
| LL1.6 Descriptive language: Uses increasingly complex sentences. | With growing interest, practices using prepositional words. For example, she says "dog inside" and then repeats "is inside" when modeled. Begins to use adverbs correctly, such as *quietly*, *loudly*, and *quickly*. For example, instead of "Nice dog" may say, "He sits nicely." | Prepositional understanding increases. Can say and act on words such as *beside*, *around*, *between*, and *over*. Uses descriptive adverbs with greater accuracy. For example, may say, "I am nicely your friend" meaning "We are playing nicely," or similar practicing of word use. | Child uses increasingly complex and varied vocabulary and language. After a nature walk, a child looks in a book about rocks and says, "This is like the rock I found under the slide." With greater accuracy uses more complex language with adverbs, prepositions, and more. |

### Anti-Bias Learning Experiences

As you plan learning experiences, consider ways to use different languages to describe the environment, behavior, and objects.

Emphasize the use of accurate vocabulary when discussing differences, avoiding favoritism or labeling. For example, "Some people choose to [do that]; others choose [the other]." Use accurate language about bodies, culture, religion, and so on.

Create learning experiences for children to practice listening. Help them learn to listen and respect others' perspectives. Provide ample time for children to share thoughts, practice words, role-play, and express themselves.

## Standard two: Emergent Reading Skills

Books are important tools for children to connect to their world and self. In books anything can be shown and shared. Children interact with the images and messages books bring to their awareness. In an anti-bias practice, we look for books that bring cultural and racial diversity messages to children. We are careful to look for books that don't take the route of "tourism." That is when cultures are represented using stereotypes as blanket definitions of the portrayed culture. Watch for gender stereotypes too. What are women and men doing in the books you share with children? Are there "good guys" and "bad guys"? What is their skin tone? Stories of empowerment, strength, and love engage children. Watch for the ways messages of "good" are built in their minds to help lay a foundation for their future of equity and justice. Often, young children will "pretend" to read or tell a story. This is not just fantasy. They are preparing for the future and using the pictures they see to make meaning of the book. Whether the work is correct is of little consequence in the grand scheme of learning to read. It is the thought connection between letters and object meaning that is significant first. Indicators of progress include the following:

- showing an interest in longer stories
- showing a personal response to the stories
- asking for stories
- anticipating story sequences
- making up words and mixing languages

Emergent readers will begin to associate sounds with words and will play with beginning and rhyming sounds. They will start to know the differences between numbers and letters and recognize the letters in their names. Both visual and auditory comprehension is necessary as children learn the skills they need to read.

| STANDARD TWO: EMERGENT READING SKILLS | | | |
|---|---|---|---|
| **Skill** | **Emerging** | **Developing** | **Proficiency** |
| LL2.1 Storytelling: Uses books and/or stories in play or otherwise. | With support, the child will sometimes join a reading circle, choose a book, and use books in play. Begins to respond personally to stories told or read aloud. For example, she considers how she might react in a similar situation to a character in the story. She could say, "I have felt [sad or happy] like [the character]," or "I say that when I am doing that too!" | Becomes more willing to be playful when reading. For example, acting out the process of reading and using character voices. Makes more and frequent connections to favorite stories. For example, at snack a child could repeat "Bread and jam for Francis!" in reference to the book. | Books are incorporated into play. Can tell the characters of the story with some assistance. Begins to enact longer stories centering self and others as characters in the stories. For example, rather than repeating key scenarios from stories in play, he makes plans for longer connected scenes to act or play out. |

| Skill | Emerging | Developing | Proficiency |
|---|---|---|---|
| LL2.2 Reading concepts: Participates in printed or oral storytelling. | Can look at a whole book front to back. Understands concepts of the story by looking through and talking about it. | Makes predictions about stories. Asks questions about stories or thinks of alternative plot twists. | Can give key details to stories. May repeat stories by heart, ask leading questions, or make "clues" to help people guess what will happen next. |
| LL2.3 Book concepts: Uses book concepts in play or otherwise. | With prompting, can repeat and answer some questions about book parts and left-to-right writing and reading. For example, practices the word *spine* in reference to book parts. | Begins to ask and answer (with less prompting) questions about book parts and left-to-right writing and reading. For example, gains familiarity with concepts such as *cover* or *title*. | Uses concepts of books such as the spine, the cover, the author, and the illustrator, to name a few. Frequently and with some support demonstrates left-to-right writing and reading in play. |
| LLS3.4 Alliteration and phonetic concepts: Plays with sound of language. | Notices that sounds make language. May say, "The car horn is talking." Practices using sounds to make words. May repeat and change word sounds. | Child begins to associate sounds with words or letters. For example, says, "Buh, buh, bird. That's B!" May make errors and persist in learning. Associates sounds with words (alliteration). Is playful with blending phonemes, alliteration, and rhyme. Makes "silly" sentences. | Understands parts of words, syllables, phonemes, and sounds. Begins to use these terms when discussing words and their parts. For example, claps syllables. Plays with words, makes new meanings. Might make "new" words or hilariously call something the "wrong" word on purpose. May make pretend words or language. |
| LL3.5 Letter awareness: Demonstrates recognition and awareness of letters. | Shows interest in letter names. For example, can find her name card with her photo as a guide. Or, picks up a name card and says, "This says 'Josie'; she's my friend." | Begins to associate letters with words. For example, he points to an *M* and says, "That says McDonalds!" With greater accuracy, names letters correctly. | Recognizes and names some letters of the alphabet, especially those in own name. May notice some shapes make letters. Child correctly names letters while playing with alphabet stamps, magnets, cards, or puzzles. With decreasing errors, names letters in the alphabet when not in alphabetic order. |

| Skill | Emerging | Developing | Proficiency |
|---|---|---|---|
| LL3.6 Vocabulary: Demonstrates word recognition and meaning. | Begins to associate words with familiar objects. For example, participates in playful vocabulary exercises during group or individual reading time, with teacher support. | More frequently, with some support, shows interest in identifying some sight words. For example, may call out the name of the sight word vocabulary card (with image) with increasing speed. | Seeks and identifies simple vocabulary words in books and other print sources. May attempt to read, point to words, and speak their meaning. May also point to words under a picture and ask, "What does that say?" |
| LL3.7 Audio discernment: Recognizes and uses sounds to communicate and interpret environment. | Child distinguishes sounds in the environment. May say she hears birds or cars, for example. | Begins to discern sounds with greater accuracy. For example, he can identify and make quiet or loud sounds. | Begins to use audio props more frequently in play. For example, may make a water sound or bird call in play. |

**Anti-Bias Learning Experiences**

Support home languages of all children in your classroom and ensure languages of all children's families are represented in the room.

Use encouragement to support all stages of reading skills. For example, make a story about an experience to share with the class.

Tell stories using word blocks, images with print, or child-made story blocks. Ensure diverse stories of culture, race, ethnicity, and roles are represented in the classroom for children to explore, and intentionally build discussions from the stories.

Make a class newsletter together. Make menus for a play restaurant. Turn a favorite story or song (or write your own as a class) into a skit or short play.

Make alphabet hopscotch to support individual's skills in annunciating letter names and sounds. Place letter cards on the floor for children to line up over the alphabet as they leave the room.

## Standard three: Emergent Writing Skills

Teachers can guide growing emergent writing skills by giving children a variety of open-ended opportunities to write freely in developmentally appropriate ways. Our teaching environments should include writing areas. We can encourage pretend writing, facilitate drawing, and start conversations about what drawings or scribblings represent. Writing opportunities should be present in all play areas too—that way, play extends to meet the learning standards easily!

Names are often the first written words children learn to recognize. No word is more important to children than their own name or the name of a loved one. Teachers can use name-recognition activities to engage children in writing. Ensure classroom environments are rich with visuals with descriptive words and options for children to mimic and write. A sign-in area gives students daily name-writing practice. You can provide the right amount of support based on their ability to hold a pencil, manipulate it, and copy the strokes letters make.

As with every domain, we can use this standard to set developmentally appropriate goals. We know that a preschooler's writing will not be school-age quality; rather it will show progress toward fluid writing. A common expectation is that a preschooler should be a great writer, like a kindergartner or even an older student. In reality, letters may be different sizes, they will likely be backward, and they may not be linear. As mastery grows, children will begin trying to write other words, and their spelling will be phonetic and not conventional. Preschoolers at the proficiency level of emergent writing will tell stories while using some written props such as signs or nametags. A child with these skills might write a somewhat discernable "M RK" on a sign meant to read, "My work." Teachers can encourage young writers with writing activities that are connected to their daily lives. These may include

- notes to parents;
- labeling work and work in progress;
- pretend food orders in dramatic play;
- scientific notes in a discovery center; and
- surveys, graphs, and charts.

| STANDARD THREE: EMERGENT WRITING SKILLS | | | |
|---|---|---|---|
| **Skill** | **Emerging** | **Developing** | **Proficiency** |
| LL3.1 Word formation: Understands letters have sounds and they make words together. | The child pretends to write words, uses writing tools in play. | Makes "letters" or "words" with shapes. Begins to understand writing perfectly "like a computer" is not usually done until children are much older. | Starts to write words such as own name and important figures. Begins to know words are used in many ways. For example, may copy letters from letter posters around the room or write "KP OT" and say, "This says, 'Keep out.'" |
| LL3.2 Letter formation: Understands letters are symbols or shapes with meaning. | Draws lines on paper. Says they are letters or people or animals, for example. Starting to write letters. Pretends to write, using drawing. A child draws or writes using pencils, markers, crayons, chalk, or paint, on paper, cardboard, or a chalkboard. | Connects or attempts to connect lines and states it is an *A*. A child writes letter-like forms on a page and says, "This is a note for my mommy." While playing restaurant, child asks, "What would you like to eat?" and scribbles the order on a pad. | Increased proficiency in making lines and shapes connect to make a real or made up "letter" on paper, chalkboard, or other material. Has increased proficiency in writing letters in name and other words of interest. |

| Skill | Emerging | Developing | Proficiency |
|---|---|---|---|
| LL3.3 Symbolic association: Connects images with meaning. | Points to a picture he drew and says, "This is my dog." Asks adult to write, "This is my dog. We went for a walk" on a drawing. She uses a variety of concept-relating items such as magazine pictures and letter stamps/symbols to make art. There is some cohesion in the thought processes. | Makes lines, shapes, or circles to write the dog's name. Thoughts become more precise when using pictures and letters/symbols to make a story or a specific picture about a real or made-up event. | Increases proficiency. For example, may deliberately practice writing the dog's name. Begins to make more complex stories, books, and graphic stories. Can tell the story and may add written or symbolic words. |

**Anti-Bias Learning Experiences**

Nurture self-confidence by documenting children's stories; also encourage children to write or draw their own stories. Explore topics of differences while documenting children's stories. Retell stories using characters and props.

Emerging writers often focus on learning to write their names. Nurture family/cultural pride by investigating where your students' names come from and what they mean.

## Standard four: Computer Knowledge

Computers, tablets, phones, and electronic toys and games are woven into the fabric of many people's lives. As with communication, the use of computer-like technology is unique to each family. Therefore children will have their own experience and understanding of what is appropriate with computers. Some children are learning to recognize and manipulate electronic devices quickly and independently while others are not. Acquiring a digital media–based vocabulary is an important building block for computer literacy. The use of "active" computer technology is not required in the preschool setting. Indeed, we think pretend play is an excellent time for teachers to introduce words and ideas that help children learn more about technology. Pretend play props that support this standard can include

- retired cell phones;
- chargers;
- old computers and keyboards;
- teacher- and student-made pretend computers; and
- radios and CD players.

Children need to mimic what they see adults doing in their lives. However, too much screen time can have a negative effect on children's brain development and executive functioning skills. The American Psychological Association (2019) updated their digital guidelines for children in an increasingly technology-rich world. We think exposure to technology is important and teachers can find creative ways to make imaginary devices and be intentional when giving children opportunities to try the real thing. Using electronic media appropriately, knowing its components, encouraging and following your students' curiosity about technology, and having limits on use are all parts of developing proficiency within this standard.

| STANDARD FOUR: COMPUTER KNOWLEDGE | | | |
|---|---|---|---|
| **Skill** | **Emerging** | **Developing** | **Proficiency** |
| LL4.1 Technology vocabulary: Demonstrates awareness of a variety of technology words. | Child shows some interest in naming devices such as tablets, cell phones, laptops, and desktop computers. With some support can use device names. For example, may incorporate the word *scanner* into dramatic play in response to peer or teacher modeling. | With increased accuracy uses devices such as play phones or computer-like technology accurately in play. For example, may use a "scanner" to search for ships at sea or to scan a bar code in a pretend store. | May create real or imaginary digital devices in play. For example, may use a paper roll to symbolize a "scanner." |
| LL4.2 Platform awareness: Demonstrates interest and awareness of technology platforms. | Begins to use names for programs and platforms used by family and community members. For example, a microwave can be "programmed" to make popcorn. | Begins to understand the purpose of programs and platforms. For example, a digital map can tell you how to get to the store. | Describes responsible uses of digital materials and technology to learn, explore, and create. Uses digital materials and technology to learn, explore, and create with the support of an adult. For example, may want to search for information on owls. |
| LL4.3 Usage awareness: Shows interest and ability in technology as a means to an end in play and otherwise. | Begins to describe the use of technological devices. For example, in play may pretend to text a friend. | Begins to discuss how devices are used, by whom, in what context. Begins to discuss ways to use digital materials to learn, explore, and create. A child may say, "Can we print that?" or "I'm putting that in my calendar." | Uses digital technology to learn, explore, and play, with adult support. Develops ideas that use computers and other digital technology to complete a project, create a game or prop, or to demonstrate learning. For example, may help print pictures to show the family. |

### Anti-Bias Learning Experiences

Recognize that each family has different access to and uses for digital technology and media. Make digital and other machine and technological devices with recyclable materials. Encourage inventions, diagrams, directions, charts, and other uses for technology. Make technology dream charts, art, and games. Support children in expressing themselves while setting limits for uses and in having equitable use of media.Use classroom media to show different areas in the world. Show and explore a new area that is very different from the culture of your classroom.

# Domain Four: Creativity and the Arts

The domain of Creativity and the Arts focuses on artistic mediums—from paper and paint to song and dance. In this domain children are communicating their thoughts and feelings through representations that use music, color, textures, and more. Its standards include the following:

1. Exploring and Expression
2. Music and Movement
3. Dramatic Play

Encouraging children to use different mediums and materials to express their thoughts and feelings is the focus of the Creativity and the Arts domain. This is an excellent opportunity to gain insight into children's awareness of themselves, their family culture, and the communities that influence their cultural identities.

Teachers can move toward anti-bias learning goals when we encourage students to celebrate their identities through artistic expression. When we show children that we respect and support their individuality, we model ways in which they can do the same for the people around them. When we appreciate diversity of thought and expression in our classrooms, our students will share in that appreciation and learn to celebrate the various contributions of their peers.

The arts and forms of dramatic play are especially rich opportunities for anti-bias learning. During play, teachers can pay close attention to the thoughts and actions of children and develop scenarios that support learning around identity, diversity, justice, and activism.

## Standard one: Exploring and Expression

Children in the emerging stage may watch others before joining in. This behavior is an effective way for the child to learn. By watching they are increasing their confidence and forming their interests. As they play more, they begin to learn the names of the media they are using and how they relate to their thoughts and emotions.

As creativity and artistic skills grow, children can integrate a greater variety of art experiences into their play. They can describe the differences in their expressions, and their detailed descriptions show an increasingly purposeful use of creative materials. For example, they may draw a tiger on a headband for a game and have specific tiger sounds and movements. Teachers can support students in acquiring these skills by remaining open and flexible to the many ways children integrate materials into play.

| STANDARD ONE: EXPLORING AND EXPRESSION | | | |
|---|---|---|---|
| **Skill** | **Emerging** | **Developing** | **Proficiency** |
| CA1.1 Expression: Uses artistic media to interact with thoughts and feelings. | Child explores an interest in art experiences. For example, may join others at the playdough table and watches intently before taking some playdough to roll. Attempts to draw or represent self or others with media ranging from movement to drawing. For example, can "move like a duck." | With some support integrates a variety of art experiences in play. For example, may add drawing to a play scenario. Begins to initiate expressive experiences. For example, she may state she is going to make herself at her birthday party in her painting. | Independently chooses art experiences. May state that he is going to paint today. With greater detail expresses self or others in work. For example, a child draws a self-portrait with most of own facial features or other details. Describes personal work. |
| CA1.2 Artistic endeavors: Shows awareness of materials used in a variety of artistic expressions. | Shows interest in understanding different art experiences such as sculpting, drawing, photography, and musical activities. May begin to seek to know names of art materials such as easel, roller brush, and dot markers. | With some support, willingly discusses differences in artistic expressions. For example, chalk is dry and washes off, and the paint is sticky on the paper. Begins to understand ways to choose which materials to use. For example, he uses sidewalk chalk outside to draw lines and "roads." | Compares elements of dance, music, theater, and visual arts, for example. Makes choices in artistic expression, depending on her desired result. Chooses several different painting tools from the art center and experiments with them. |
| CA1.3 Emotional expression (imagery): Associates images with concepts such as feelings. | Uses art as an expression of self. For example, paints abstractly and when asked names it as "his park" or any other object or scenario of interest. Connects feelings to art such as "sad" or "excited." | Begins to more frequently and with less prompting tell a story about the picture she drew. May cover the painting with black paint because "it is nighttime." Is purposeful when describing emotions in art. | Revises creative work using feedback. For example, might add new elements to work after sharing thoughts about its meaning to make it clearer. |

| Skill | Emerging | Developing | Proficiency |
|---|---|---|---|
| CA1.4 Visual patterns: Engages in visual patterning with interest. | Notices patterns in art expressions. Makes patterns with color and shapes. | Attempts to make unique patterns with color and shapes. | More proficient in attempts to make unique patterns with color and shapes. |

**Anti-Bias Learning Experiences**

Provide children opportunities to learn about creative expression in different cultures. The children's individual family cultures and broader community cultures are good places to start. Ensure your creative materials represent different skin tones and hair colors, and include a variety of media, textures, and colors for children to explore.

Encourage confidence by giving lots of opportunities to enjoy open-ended projects where children can take risks and have fun!

## Standard two: Music and Movement

For many people, music and movement are important cultural touchstones, as evidenced in research conducted by Williams and Berthelsen (2018, 2019). At the YWCA, we think movement and music learning is an essential part of high-quality teaching. Music and movement often speak to the heart of a person. People all over the world use movement and music to express their feelings and tell stories. What an incredibly important aspect of the human experience! As children's music and movement skills develop, they will begin to create their own dances, describe what they hear, and respond to different musical sounds. As development continues, children will be able to march and keep time with the beat.

A musical showcase of children's families' favorite songs can be an exciting way to connect to home lives and encourage creative development. Ms. Dianne talked about using home music to help children express themselves creatively. "One of my favorite things to ask children is about the song they have in their head. I've also asked parents at drop-off if they had music playing this morning or if they sang a song. I noticed with one family they began to pay attention to the music in their lives. Adrianna began keeping a list of all 'her songs' in our room." Creating simple musical instruments like shakers and drums can give students the tools they need to practice their skills. Children show mastery of this standard when they can demonstrate the following:

- helping others learn how to use instruments
- helping others learn to dance and sing
- using instruments such as maracas, rattles, rain sticks, or tambourines to help keep time or create a rhythm
- using body movements to express emotion and pretend play

| | | STANDARD TWO: MUSIC AND MOVEMENT | | |
|---|---|---|---|
| Skill | Emerging | Developing | Proficiency |
| CA2.1 Movement usage: Recognizes movement can be used to show meaning. | Begins to use music or percussion to describe feelings. For example, "This is my excited bear-hunt clap." | Child adds additional "moves" to planned dance or routine. Might "lead" yoga, choosing star, triangle, or dog pose, for example. Child can march, keeping time with the beat with teachers or peers modeling. | Uses song and music in play. Uses sound to show feeling. Sings the bear-hunt song and dings a bell when it's time to "be scared," for example. Follows dance or movement routines with little support. |
| CA2.2 Dance: Uses dance to show thoughts and feelings. | Shows interest in and attempts to follow guided dances. | Participates in planning multi-step rhythm or dance with support and recites planned or learned routines. | Teaches others a dance. Participates in learning new movements. |
| CA2.3 Emotional expression (tonal): Recognizes sounds can have meaning. | Begins to use sound to represent concepts. Can use a pretend cooking pan for a drum, for example. | Begins to equate more feelings with sounds. For example, "That sounds like happy fishies swimming." | Describes sounds with a personal, emotional connection. Might say, "This is my happy voice!" |
| CA2.4 Instrument knowledge: Develops awareness of musical instruments. | Explores instruments. Tries a variety of play instruments and finds a favorite. | Thinks about how instruments work. For example, uses a carton and rocks to make a percussion instrument. | Using maracas, rattles, rain sticks, or tambourine, the child keeps time with the music. |

**Anti-Bias Learning Experiences**

Learn families' favorite songs and use them in daily classroom life. Seek the connections that families have to music and be overt about the specific types of music being played; name the music and make the connection.

Explore reasons for music such as celebrations or other occasions, the civil rights movement, faiths and religions, or historical events.

Explore different instruments and dances and have children create new instruments to make music and dance.

## Standard three: Dramatic Play

Children engaged in dramatic play will carefully watch and listen to see how others are playing. Emergent learners may agree to take an easy role. For example, they might pretend to be the baby of the family.

As this skill develops, children will add complexity to their pretend play, using costumes and props. They take on more complex roles too. They might be a doctor with a notepad, writing notes about what they see with their patient; a server taking your food order at a restaurant; or a hairdresser doing hair and nails. Keep in mind that children's pretending will reflect their life experiences; at times children may role-play scenarios that reflect trauma or other negative incidents they have experienced.

Children need help to master this skill because play is a learned activity as well as a natural impulse. Meaghan Elizabeth Taylor and Wanda Boyer (2020) remind us that the concept of play-based learning is woven through major child development theories. It is often said that "Play is the work of children," and we completely agree. Through interest and attention to action, children learn skills that are both social and preacademic. In other words, when children are curious, they examine the object of curiosity. Through these interactions, they begin to notice more and more how what they do makes an impact on the object of interest. As they grow, they can learn that what they do may influence the environment, their awareness, and the awareness and experiences of people in their sphere. In this way they can begin to place themselves in relationship with others. Experiencing the effect of one's actions on the self and others leads to deeper curiosity about other phenomena in the world. Play leads children to witness their impact as well as their ability to self-select inquiry into the world around them.

Dramatic play is sometimes simply called pretending. Adults will recall when they "lost track of time" as a child or "forgot the world" during play. The freedom to choose play is, we think, one of the foundational aspects of an anti-bias educational environment. We think this can be the place where we begin to build the free, fair, and just world we want to see. We love when children make their own stories and wholeheartedly encourage it. Pretend play might not yet include other children—a child may prefer alternatives to people, such as a doll, for example. As a teacher, it is key to watch for repetitive play scenarios and find ways to "complicate" them. For example, if children are repeatedly mewing like a kitten, we might roll them a pretend ball of yarn and help them bat it about. Then we might suggest that the kittens go for a walk and see what they can find. When children master this skill, they are ready to be on stage! They can perform for others and remember the details of their stories for days. They can pick up where they left off and add to the story they are inventing as time goes on.

| STANDARD THREE: DRAMATIC PLAY | | | |
|---|---|---|---|
| **Skill** | **Emerging** | **Developing** | **Proficiency** |
| CA3.1 Character development: Uses characters to express thoughts and feelings. | CA3.1 Character development: Uses characters to express thoughts and feelings. | Follows roles associated with clothes worn in dress-up. For example, he may want to be called the name of his character and behave in ways that show that character's mannerisms. | Characters are developed for the purpose of play. She may ask for or make symbols to wear in play. For example, she makes a headband of construction paper with a tiger drawing to be a tiger. |

| Skill | Emerging | Developing | Proficiency |
|---|---|---|---|
| CA3.2 Role development: Associates roles with characters based on desired outcomes. | Participates in role-playing with prompting and guidance. For example, she can be a barber when reminded to wash and cut hair, have the customer pay, and then sweep up. | Follows instructions/prompts for roles and actions to take and then becomes engrossed and inventive within the role. Makes or follows suggestions to make the game complex. For example, what happens if two customers come in at the same time? Or what if there is not enough change in the till? | Plays the story throughout the day or across days. Adds to the game, such as by making play money for the till or creating a list of services or adding daily specials. |
| CA3.3 Intentional play: Develops structure to play scenarios. | Shows interest in play planning. Child agrees to play a role but waits for directions. She may listen independently or with support as plans unfold. | Independently, or with some assistance, offers thoughts and suggestions for play planning. | Creates a play or story with friends. He may extend the story-play though the day or across days. |
| CA3.4 Decision-making: Makes choices in play scenarios to achieve a desired outcome. | Repeats actions in play. For example, walking in and out of the "house," going to work and coming home, or being a baby crying. Agrees to be the kitty and sits quietly on the chair. Will "meow" or "eat" with prompting. | With support, adds to play. For example, in addition to leaving and returning "home," may pretend to drive/bus/walk to work. May make a meal as an adult, as a kitten may find string to play with, or as a baby, learn to walk and talk. | Adds to stories with plots and plans. For example, the kittens have ideas and leave the house or make a game. Reminds friends which characters they played yesterday so they can continue today. |

**Anti-Bias Learning Experiences**

Include props and materials in the dramatic play learning center that reflect the everyday life experiences of the children as well as experiences that may be new to them.

Promote culture, gender, race, religion, and ability equity in socio-dramatic play. Guide play by asking challenging questions about roles and expectations.

Provide devoted time to play planning. Make mind maps, lists, and charts to show children's ideas and interest in play. Document work and showcase the imaginative development of children.

# Domain Five: Mathematical Development

Mathematical development is a complex domain wherein teachers guide students to recognize patterns, shapes, spatial relationships, and design. Children also develop an understanding of number vocabulary, correlation, counting, mathematical operations, and measuring.

This domain has three standards:

1. Numerals and Patterns
2. Measurement
3. Geometry, Spatial Thinking, and Data Analysis

Anti-bias goals can be set in every domain, and math is no exception. Anti-bias teachers constantly look for ways to encourage positive identity formation and an appreciation for diversity. We can always look for opportunities to identify fair and unfair situations. Using the concepts "more" and "less," we can investigate fairness and equity. As children learn to discriminate shapes, colors, and numbers, we can watch for cues that they are noticing human differences and help them develop an accurate vocabulary to express this learning. During a skin tone paint-mixing activity, teachers Ms. Hannah and Ms. Fowsia helped children count how many parts of each color they were using. Later, on the diversely toned handprint "rainbow" they hung in the hall, children's names also had a math equation for the colors each child used next to it. Beside Hennessey's name, for example, was B3+Y1+W2, which stood for three parts brown, one part yellow, and two parts white paint. We can also pick out learning tools that support mathematical development *and* anti-bias learning. For example, puzzles can celebrate diversity by depicting multicultural characters.

## Standard one: Numerals and Patterns

With developmentally appropriate expectations, teachers lead children to use number and pattern language correctly and with increasing frequency. Numerical vocabulary can be incorporated into play and included in group conversations.

Emergent learners can demonstrate one-to-one correspondence between objects and recognize numbers up to five. They might point out and count the buttons on their shirt or count beads as they string them onto a necklace. They strive to recite numbers in order up to ten. Development continues as children learn to name numbers up to twenty-nine, increase their observation of numerals in their environment, and describe the attributes of objects. Proficiency is seen when children display fluidity and correctness in counting up to twenty or higher.

Patterning is an area that teachers sometimes overlook when guiding mathematical skill building. We can target our teaching by encouraging children to sort objects based on characteristics: first one attribute, and later more than one, like color, size, and shape. We can guide them to notice, copy, and describe patterns both seen and heard.

Development continues as students copy patterns and show that they are thinking critically about what they are seeing and hearing. Proficiency comes when children are able to build their own patterns and extend that pattern by showing or telling what comes next.

Graphing or charting on paper with the children is another activity that supports analytical thinking, which is critical to cognitive development. Children who try to read a graph or chart are showing development in this standard. One teacher, Mr. Juan, described his use of an interactive emotion chart to help children equate numerical words to meaning. The chart had many emotions with cartoon faces showing various expressions. Each child had an envelope with their face and name on several small tags. The tags were attached to the chart using Velcro tabs. Multiple children could occupy an emotion category together, and each child could be represented by several emotions at one time. During snack the group would discuss how their emotions moved throughout the day and counted the transitions they had gone though. This is a way that individuality and diversity is connected to meaningful activities that support the development of early mathematical skills.

| STANDARD ONE: NUMERALS AND PATTERNS | | | |
|---|---|---|---|
| Skill | Emerging | Developing | Proficiency |
| MD1.1 Numeral awareness: Uses numeral vocabulary. | The child uses number images, not necessarily correctly. May name a number in the room incorrectly or ask, "What number is that?" when the teacher is marking the daily attendance. | More accurately notices and uses numbers in play. For example, may tell another the name of the numeral on their shirt or stand on the number four square when prompted. | Increased use of correctly stated numbers in order backward and forward. For example, counts down from ten or twenty to start a race. May count out loud for fun. |
| MD1.2 Pattern organization: Groups concepts or ideas based on criteria or number. | Organizes objects based on single concepts. May put a set of objects together based on one characteristic (color, size, or shape). | Groups objects using multiple characteristics. For example, chooses paintbrushes that are yellow and thin. | Becomes more aware and precise in complex ordering, such as "three people are on the bikes; they all chose blue bikes with three wheels!" |
| MD1.3 Sequencing: Recognition of numerical patterns. | Understands sequencing. Might laugh when someone says "one, two, banana!" rather than "one, two, three." | Can fill in missing numbers. For example, in circle time teachers count the days of the week, intentionally skipping a number. Child notices and states the missing number. | Helps others sequence numbers. May wait for others to answer correctly before saying their answer to give others a chance. |

| Skill | Emerging | Developing | Proficiency |
|---|---|---|---|
| MD1.4 Numeral representation: Makes numerals with a variety of media. | Represents numbers. For example, pretends to write numbers in play, drawing lines in sand and saying they are numbers. | More accurately represents numbers using writing utensils or other media. With some assistance develops an interest in making numbers at the playdough table, for example. | Can verbalize, signal, or write up to ten. For example, can shape a zero with string or write with a marker. |
| MD1.5 One-to-one correspondence: Attaches numerical value to objects or concepts. | Begins to understand one-to-one correspondence. For example, may "count" items in play using objects, body movements, or sounds. | Begins to demonstrate more precise counting. For example, may give everyone two crackers or take turns kicking a ball three times. | Growing proficiency with one-to-one correspondence. For example, looks at the class graph of favorite fruits. The child says, "seven of us like grapes." |
| MD1.6 Patterns and Categories: Organizes concepts of grouping actions or objects in play or otherwise. | Child can copy a short clapping pattern like clap, clap-clap, clap, clap-clap. Attempts to guess when asked to sort objects based on attributes. | With support, applies a rule to patterns: a child copies the teacher's pattern with red and yellow blocks using a different color such as blue and green. With greater autonomy and accuracy sorts objects based on attributes. | Adds to or subtracts from patterns. For example, may line up all the zebras and giraffes in a pattern, describe it, and then reorganize based on different attributes. A child sorts objects into more abstract categories such as "sinks" or "floats." May make suggestions such as "This side of the room should stomp their feet and that side clap" in a rhythm game. |

**Anti-Bias Learning Experiences**
Making maps or dioramas of children's homes, rooms, cities, or towns are good opportunities to connect shapes with individual cultural similarities and differences.

## Standard two: Measurement

Many preschool-age children are very interested in asking, finding, measuring, and describing conditions using terms such as *how much*, *when*, and *what*. When a child gives her friend a pile of blocks and says, "Now you have more!" she is learning to measure. Teachers can guide development by encouraging students to collect objects like rocks, sort them, and categorize them. As this skill increases, children will use more complex descriptions of the rocks to measure them. For example, they might begin by sorting the rocks by the number, then by color, size, and finally, surface texture.

## STANDARD TWO: MEASUREMENT

| Skill | Emerging | Developing | Proficiency |
|---|---|---|---|
| MD2.1 Quantity and order: Demonstrates interest and awareness of amounts. | Shows interest in measuring. For example, asks for more bubbles in the water table and uses her hands to show the estimated amount she wants. Conceptualizes quantity and order. For example, may question if he has more or less of a coveted object. | Is more accurate in measurement. Can with some assistance pour half a cup of sand in the sensory table. Begins to realize that after first comes second. For example, sighs and crosses arms and grumbles, "I'm not first! I'll go next." | Initiates measuring. Shows interest in counting chairs at the table, puzzles on the shelf, or any object of interest. Begins to name positions and qualities more accurately. May say, "The first scoop was me. Now it's your turn to try." |
| MD2.2 Dimensional Awareness: Participates in description and use of size, distance, and volume concepts. | Shows interest in height, width, distance, or dimension. For example, participates in measuring feet in an "all about me" exercise. | With some assistance, considers size awareness with objects outside of the self. For example, when encouraged, counts the number of steps backward he can take and still hit the paper with the water when squirting a spray bottle outside. | With greater independence discerns differences in size, shape, or distance. For example, may exclaim that her painting is bigger than another's. |
| MD2.3 Time concepts: Expresses concepts placed in time. | With some support, talks about beginning, middle, and end of a time span. May say, "It's almost time to go home." Uses some references to time, not necessarily accurately, in play or conversation. | With more independence will reference past or future experiences. For example, may say, "I went to my grandma's house" but be less clear regarding when exactly in the past this event occurred. | With greater skill accurately names a specific timeline of events. May say, for example, "When I am five, I will go to kindergarten" or "When I was a grown-up, I went on a vacation." |

### Anti-Bias Learning Experiences

Use a play kitchen, grocery store, or restaurant to expose children to different ways of measurement. Use found objects like sticks or string to measure, make a scale, and so on. Encourage all children to participate in the roleplay opportunities, regardless of traditional gender roles. Encourage traditional, invented, and all kinds of food that are real to or made-up by children.

Explore ways of counting and valuing. For example, why do we call them "inches" and "feet"? Do people measure weight and length differently in our world? Can you make your own unit of measurement? For example, what if a "one" was equal to "One giant step"?

Talk about more, less, and equal in the context of fairness or equity with food, toys, and other everyday materials. For example, in a gardening project, not all plants need the same support to grow. Can you chart the growth of plants?

Ask families for recipes. Cooking experiences are excellent mathematical opportunities. In a field, like math, which is traditional male dominated, this is a great opportunity to emphasize how much math is used in traditional "women's work," like cooking, while also encouraging boys to explore cook.

Remember that preschool children are playing with the concepts they will learn to use more accurately in higher grades. It is appropriate for a preschooler to say "when I was a grown-up" if they want to imagine what they might do when they are older.

## Standard three: Geometry, Spatial Thinking, and Data Analysis

Growth in the third math standard happens when children learn about geometry, show spatial awareness, and begin to understand and interpret data. They grow in these skills through trial and error, and we may observe them trying a variety of methods to achieve desired results.

Puzzles are a common way to learn geometry and spatial awareness. Puzzle play promotes actions like trial and error, turning objects to make them fit, and noticing outline shapes. As children learn that shapes have names and commonalities, they may independently identify common shapes like circles, triangles, and squares in their environment. They may use shapes in play and creative art. A child at this stage might make a square on a simple map to show her house. Children master this standard when they can name shapes and begin to recognize more complex shapes, like trapezoid, hexagon, column, pyramid, cone, or cube. In addition, they can use shapes to represent concepts and ideas during play, art, or storytelling.

Teachers should remember to use their self-reflective skills in this area to help promote anti-bias thinking and teaching. For example, Ms. Nichole reported feeling frustrated that some children did not seem interested in learning the names of shapes beyond simple and common squares, circles, and triangles. In a self-reflective session, she explored some of the thoughts she had about her expectations for children's learning in this area. Upon deeper reflection, she realized she was worried about kindergarten readiness, even though the standard for preschoolers does not include accurate knowledge of trapezoids and cylinders. However, being able to construct and deconstruct shapes *is* a goal for older preschoolers. So Ms. Nichole focused her efforts on what children were interested in by taking notes on conversations and stories the children shared during the day with her and each other. Ms. Nichole put effort into observing her class, with a plan to connect her class's interest with both learning standards and anti-bias teaching goals.

"The boys are obsessed with superheroes right now," she reported to her co-teacher Ms. Kenya. "I don't react well to this; it supports violence, and that is against our policy. I have to find a way to reduce this fight between our rules and their interests." After some brainstorming, the teachers decided to bring the issue to the class. They told the group that the superhero play was worrisome to them because "We want to support peace and are afraid we are seeing too much fighting. How can we support peace?" Through discussion, the group affirmed their wish for peace as well and they reminded the teachers that as superheroes they *were* fighting for peace. The group made a "Plan for Peace" that included making "Hero Tools" rather than weapons out of recycled cardboard boxes and paper rolls. The teachers documented the construction projects as children pulled apart shapes and glued and taped them together. In the final presentation board, children made shape keys that showed how many different shapes went into the design of their Hero Tool. One child's Hero Tool looked like this:

**2 + 1 =**

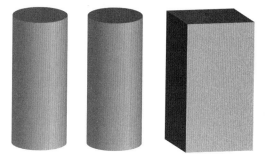

Concepts of directions, proximity, and location, such as "near" or "far" are included in this standard. Accuracy and complexity increases as these skills are developed. Children show their proficiency when they understand how to move their bodies in relation to space. They know when they are standing "next to" or "behind" something. The superheroes in Ms. Nicole and Ms. Kenya's class practiced this concept with paper roll binoculars in their revised Plan for Peace Hero Play. This is an example of how relevant play and interest can be leveraged to support mathematical skills while supporting individual interests and perspectives of each child.

When analyzing data, children participate in collecting information and making sense out of it. For example, they may describe the shapes and sizes of a pile of leaves as a triangle. As children develop, these considerations become more complex, and children can begin to make their own charts and graphs.

| STANDARD THREE: GEOMETRY, SPATIAL THINKING, AND DATA ANALYSIS | | | |
|---|---|---|---|
| **Skill** | **Emerging** | **Developing** | **Proficiency** |
| MD3.1 Shapes knowledge: Demonstrates interest in using shapes and shape words. | The child notices shapes in the environment. May see how the cut tree is a circle. | Begins to understand parts of shapes. For example, with some support, can take a cardboard box apart to notice two of the sides are different shapes. | Understands shapes can be built or taken apart. May say, "Let's cut this square in half so we have two halves." May be interested in related terms such as *semicircle*. |
| MD3.2 Spatial awareness: Interacts with objects in space. | Awareness of space. May try to fit a peg in a hole or fit the toy truck in a "parking space" under a chair. | Recognizes placement of objects. For example, may state the bikes do not go on the climber because "they won't fit." | Reminds self or others to turn puzzle pieces until they fit. |

| Skill | Emerging | Developing | Proficiency |
|---|---|---|---|
| MD3.3 Distance and location: Demonstrates consideration of location of self or objects in time and space. | Shows interest in location. May practice using location words and matching actions, such as moving her body under the climber or throwing the ball over the bucket. | Begins to share information about distance. May say "We waited a long time; we were last" or "My uncle lives seventy-five [arbitrary] miles away." | Comprehends distance more accurately. Can explain how maps may be used, for instance. |
| MD3.4 Data analysis: Visually represents concepts of interest. | Shows interest in charts and graphs about pertinent subjects. For example, tells a room visitor there is a chart to show how many children love trucks or cars. | Uses graphs or charts to play. May keep real or pretend score in the Olympics races she is playing that week. | Considers data. Can talk about collected information. Can share that every child tried a new food this week by looking at a chart. |

**Anti-Bias Learning Experiences**
Use cloth, textures, patterns, and materials that are familiar to children to explain shapes, patterns, and analysis. Sharing favorite objects from home can open a conversation about geometry, for example.

Use charts, graphs, and maps made by the class to show information of interest, such as favorite foods, hair length, or eye color. Make a chart with your class of the things you can pretend to play. This allows you to list what children's favorite concepts are and make plans to bring in materials for the play stations that will deepen imaginative and immersive play.

# Domain Six: Scientific Thinking

Scientific thinking is a process. The process of thinking scientifically, rather than prede-termining a particular outcome, is most important for preschoolers in the development of this skill.

This domain has just one standard, Discover, Act, and Apply Strategies, which describes the cycle of inquiry.

Sometimes we hear teachers say, "I'm not good at science," meaning they probably did not feel that they excelled in high school chemistry. "Doing science" does not have to mean setting up elaborate experiments with safety goggles and bubbling liquid—though there are plenty of ways to use household items for some exciting and safe chemical reactions! Even without chemical reactions, early scientific-thinking skills are first developed in a cycle of inquiry. When children ask "why" or "what if," we think it is the teacher's job to wonder right along with them and find ways to find out. Alison Gopnik (2012) clearly shows that preschoolers are capable of very complex scientific thinking. She reports that children use scientific thinking like hypotheses and theories to solve real problems, and they can analyze and measure statistics too. To Gopnik, if adults assume that children are not engaged in deep and critical thinking, they can miss the opportunity to foster greater learning. We have found that preschoolers ask questions, make plans and predictions, and express their findings. We see it when a face lights up in understanding or with a big

idea. We hear it when children describe what they were playing and how they solved a problem.

Gopnik thinks children were built for scientific inquiry. She thinks that adults can learn a lot about learning by supporting the inquisitiveness of children and not dismissing play as just silliness. Lin Bian, Sarah-Jane Leslie, and Andrei Cimpian (2018) found that bias against women in science and regarding intelligence in general may start in children's early years. The researchers found that both boys and girls favored boys when selecting teammates for a fabricated game that required people to have stereotypical definitions of intelligence such as a high IQ. Although the study was conducted with children between the ages of five and seven, we think the fact that girls were not chosen as teammates by both boys and girls tells us this kind of bias may begin early, so that is when we must address it and try to stop it. We think that when caregivers send messages to young children that all people are able to be geniuses, children develop powerful self-images as well as a willingness to embark on risky learning experiences that involve making guesses and sharing one's thoughts.

Ms. Kathy had a basic solution she liked to use with her preschool children. She played a game with them by calling them "Doctor" and adding their name after. All the children began referring to themselves as Doctor in her room, and many play explorations resulted. When conducting experiments with color mixing, for example, each Doctor would offer a "hypothesis." In this scenario, all children were held to a high standard. Walter Gilliam and colleagues (2016) studied how teachers struggle with holding the same high standards for all children. This study found uneven expectations regarding children's behavior based on both the race of the teacher and of the children.

One way we can combat the unconscious building of negative stereotypes is by including children in planning and developing activities. Ms. Dianne remembered a time in her class where she asked the group what their favorite things were. She said the answers were everywhere from chocolate chips to dinosaurs, ponytails, and binoculars. "We designed games and play scenarios that we built together. It was much more fun to make a cardboard dinosaur and giant cookie circle squares together than it would have been to hand premade items to the children. I think they care more about the process of getting to the end of the game than the game itself," she said. We think the process is the game and children can be part of it.

# Standard one: Discover, Act, and Apply Strategies

The act of scientific discovery uses the following skills:

- noticing differences and similarities in environments, objects, and materials
- looking for evidence to support understanding
- using simple tools

In the emerging phase of scientific thinking, children make simple plans of action. They begin to predict outcomes. Emerging scientific thinkers consider a variety of solutions and look for evidence to support their understanding. As scientific-thinking skills develop further, children can pose more complex questions and investigate carefully using their knowledge, experience, and tools. A child might try to add blocks to a bin and say, "This doesn't fit!" When asked to solve the problem, they decide to take some out.

Teachers can guide learning in this domain by providing opportunities to investigate weather, space, bodies of water, velocity, and gravity. As standards are being mastered, scientific thinkers will compare what they observe in nature with other reports. Children will begin to understand that the sun is a source of heat and light or describe why it rains. A child may say, "It's hot, so we can bring water and read outside?" Children can explain complex reasoning and understand that their reasons are different from another person's. A student achieving mastery in scientific thinking could, at this point, take a ramp made of a wooden plank and turn it into a fence, or suggest ways to repair something, like a loose cabinet or broken toy.

Anti-bias teachers find every opportunity to encourage and affirm scientific thinking. Our classrooms are filled with "what if" questions and "imagine this" conversations as children achieve mastery. Our developing scientists are building the skills they need to be critical thinkers and thoughtful activists as they begin to make plans in advance, take other ideas into consideration, and compare possible outcomes. They can make fair decisions and change plans as needed to accommodate the needs of others.

| STANDARD ONE: DISCOVER, ACT, AND APPLY STRATEGIES | | | |
|---|---|---|---|
| **Skill** | **Emerging** | **Developing** | **Proficiency** |
| ST1.1 Phenomena awareness: Demonstrates curiosity and interest in differences between phenomena. | The child notices differences. May describe unique characteristics in the environment, such as "I was grumpy before breakfast; now I'm better," or "My blanket is yellow; yours is green." | Begins to develop ideas about why things are different from one another. For example, may look closely at rocks and ask why one rock is grey and another is brown. May ask why the sky is blue or make jokes that it is not blue. | Becomes more detailed in describing differences. Starts to point out differences or look for answers to phenomena. May struggle to resolve apparent contradictions, such as why the yellow sun doesn't make the sky yellow too. |

| Skill | Emerging | Developing | Proficiency |
|---|---|---|---|
| ST1.2 Questioning: Tests hypotheses and asks questions. | Makes questions during play. For example, in a game where the grass is "lava," finds a sled so they can all get to safety. Is more willing to try again when building ramps for cars to roll down. Notices the red car turns in one direction and that the ramps are uneven in texture. | Makes more questions in play and conversations that relate to life. For example, pretends a stuffed toy is "sick" and gives it "medicine" to feel better. Talks through ideas before trying them. For example, says, "If we use a towel on the slide, it will dry. We will have to wash the towel later." May suggest another towel if the slide is not dry enough after using the first one. | Has complicated ideas about why things are as they seem. For example, she may say the grass is pokey on her feet because it has sticks growing in it. The complex thinking does not need to be correct; rather it shows a creative and curious mind. Thinks ahead to a solution. For example, may say, "[The idea] will not work and we need to do [this] because I tried it before." |
| ST1.3 Action: Explores phenomena of interest. | Spends longer periods of time working and playing with things that are interesting to her. For example, may insist on playing in the same area many days in a row. Practices "washing clothes" in a basin labeled with a drawing and the word "washing machine." | Looks for more information about things that are interesting. For example, he likes dolls and especially their hair. He talks about hair, is happy to have a book about hair, and draws hair on his self-portrait. Wants to set up a pretend salon. Has a hairbrush, dryer, or towel, and uses them accurately. Can be inventive when the correct tools are lacking. | Hypothesizes about phenomena. For example, in a discussion about food preferences, wonders out loud if the food we eat changes our skin color, "like flamingos are pink from their food," then holds a magnifying glass up to her hand to "see" what she ate for dinner yesterday. |
| ST1.4 Nature awareness: Expresses interest in and recognition of the natural world. | Begins to question nature and the difference between human and nature-made phenomena. For example, compares a lake to a swimming pool or mixes the words and concepts up. | Asks many questions about natural and human-made experiences. For example, asks why it rains, where the wind comes from, or why the sun is hot. | Can accurately describe some natural phenomena. For example, might say, "The volcano is sleeping" or "Storms are sometimes far away and sometimes close." |

**Anti-Bias Learning Experiences**

Use materials that are representative of the children in your room, such as a rock collection from the local neighborhood.

Collect natural phenomena and creation stories from children's ethnic cultures. Discuss the origins of the sun, moon, and wind from different folklore perspectives.

Deliberately refer to children as scientists and ask for hypotheses. Use scientific words and make charts showing each child's predictions and ideas.

# Domain Seven: Physical and Motor Development

As young children learn to move their bodies with balance, accuracy, and control, they build confidence and self-awareness. This learning supports our anti-bias goal to help each child build a positive social identity. As children engage physically with the world in big and small ways, we can help them notice how their actions affect those around them. We can show them how to be respectful of other people's bodies. This will reinforce their ability to form deep, caring human connections with their peers.

This domain's standards are as follows:

1. Large-Motor Skills
2. Fine-Motor Skills
3. Healthy and Safe Living Practices

## Standard one: Large-Motor Skills

Some of children's most expressive moments come when they are moving their bodies. From walking and hopping to running, climbing, and throwing, children seem built to move. Not all children move the same, yet all movement contributes to physical development and large-motor skills. When muscles and coordination are developing, children sometimes need assistance. For example, a student might need encouragement to try crawling under objects in an obstacle course. Children can use handrails or hand supports to walk on ramps.

Emerging large-motor skills often mean children can manage stairs with assistance. Children at this stage also enjoy climbing on and off furniture. They can coordinate a two-footed jump, throw a ball at a target, and try to get on a swing.

As children become more competent, they need less verbal or physical support to use their bodies. Ramps and stairs are managed independently. Children enjoy climbing but may not get to the very top or know how to get down alone. They begin to hop on one foot, kick, throw and catch balls, and pedal on riding toys. They begin to move in and out of spaces independently.

Proficiency comes differently to all children. It is an important part of an anti-bias practice to remember that proficiency in movement is not categorically the same. Expecting everyone to reach the same level of ability is one form of ableism. For example, if teachers are athletic, how do they adjust their expectations to honor and support the individual abilities of each child? Do they keep pressing children to kick the ball like the student that most closely matches an ideal of physical skill and ability, or do they encourage each child to improve their own kicking skills?

Teachers who provide opportunities to practice and build confidence can support growth. They can give their students chances to balance, manage stairs, jump from different heights, gallop, pump their legs on a swing, use a pedal toy, and kick, catch, and throw smaller objects. Remember, every student has their own physical ability level; this is especially important to note for children with physical and mental disabilities, whose progress may look very different. Gender expectations can also affect the messages teachers make about physicality. Rohan Telford and colleagues (2016) found girls were less encouraged than boys to be physically active. Dawn Heinecken (2020) explored and acknowledged there are difficult intersections between race and gender in the world of sports. There are stereotypes about what people can and cannot do based on ethnicity, gender, race, and ability—all a part of today's complex setting that our curriculum hopes to help us address. For example, in conversation about physical activity, Ms. Tanya shared a story about her memory of play as a child. She said she was in many sports growing up and could now see she valued physical skills and ability very highly. "I think I was expecting all children to love moving as much as I did," she said. "I was feeling very frustrated with children who did not want to run and jump with me outside. Our curriculum reminded me that my way of approaching activity is not the same for all people. I really focus on girls playing and have felt frustrated when some children, boys or girls, have not been excited to play games like those I liked as a child. I have a lot of learning to do to help me and all of us understand what proficiency looks like for each child."

## STANDARD ONE: LARGE-MOTOR SKILLS

| Skill | Emerging | Developing | Proficiency |
|---|---|---|---|
| PM1.1 Intentional movement: Moves with increasing purpose and precision. | The child crawls under and over a variety objects and climbs off and on furniture. Is beginning to understand how to move in and out of spaces. May ask for help climbing up or down from a climber. | With greater skill, manages to climb and crawl on stairs, equipment, and a variety of objects. For example, child enjoys climbing but hasn't climbed to the very top of the equipment yet. | Enjoys obstacle courses. Repeatedly and with different actions, tries new ways of climbing and crawling. Initiates movement experiences. May say, "I am going to slide down the pole." |
| PM1.2 Balance: Uses core strength to move body. | Can walk on a slightly inclined surface with assistance. Manages stairs with assistance. | With less assistance, can walk or run on a slightly inclined surface. | Walks with balance along narrow surfaces such as curbs, balance beams, or lines. Can walk up and down stairs holding the handrail. |
| PM1.3 Leg coordination: Uses legs with increasing accuracy to move the body. | Practices jumping, though may not jump with both feet together yet. Practices kicking with increasing accuracy. | Jumps with two feet or hops on one foot. Kicks a medium-sized ball; throws a large ball with two hands. Begins pushing riding toys with feet and later begins pedaling. | Can jump from varied heights. Skips, kicks, and gallops. May be inventive with movement. Explores ways to run and walk such as walking backward or running around the perimeter of the playground. |

| Skill | Emerging | Developing | Proficiency |
|---|---|---|---|
| PM1.4 Arm coordination: Uses arms purposefully with increasing accuracy. | Child throws a ball to a friend. | Starts to catch using two hands, as if catching a football. | Child throws small and large objects to practice catching. Throws smaller balls with some accuracy. Bounces and catches larger balls. |

**Anti-Bias Learning Experiences**

How do children move at home? Do they dance, play games, or walk? Seek ways to represent ways of moving that children are familiar with.

Be explicit in supportively communicating differences in physical skills, ability, and appearance with children.

Use "personal best" charts to show individual competency growth.

Make treasure maps and obstacle courses. Encourage children to design movement games, dances, and actions.

## Standard two: Fine-Motor Skills

Standard two focuses on coordinating hand-eye movement or dexterity and strengthening the small muscles of the hands. Teachers encourage development when they give students the chance to use their hands to play and perform self-care. From sensory tables and scissors to zippers and snaps, small muscles need a lot of practice to get strong!

As fine-motor control continues to develop, writing tools are held between two fingers in a pincer grip rather than in a fisted grip. Hammering with toys, using scissors, stacking blocks, stringing smaller beads, completing puzzles, drawing, and using chopsticks are examples of activities that support the development of fine-motor skills.

Proficiency is found when the eyes and hands work together easily and muscle strength is increased. Children at this level can use a three-hole punch correctly and handle scissors fluidly, and when getting dressed or undressed they snap, button, and zip. More details emerge in their drawings, and given regular opportunities to paint, mature painting skills will be evident—colors will be less muddy and images less abstract. Young artists add new details to drawings, and storytelling art will emerge. They may include additions that symbolize fantasy or mimic real details or events.

As with all skills, teachers focus understanding development based on a child's individual level and take family culture into account when interpreting skills. For example, in families where children are fed by older caregivers through most of infancy and toddlerhood, using eating utensils may not only be difficult for the eyes and hand muscles to coordinate, but the concept may also take getting used to. Or, if children are often helped by older caregivers in their home to undress and toilet, learning to pull pants and snap may be a physical and mental challenge that takes time.

| STANDARD TWO: FINE-MOTOR SKILLS | | | |
|---|---|---|---|
| **Skill** | **Emerging** | **Developing** | **Proficiency** |
| PM2.1 Hand strength: With increasing skill uses finger and hand strength to perform tasks. | Child engages in activities that require finger strength. For example, tries to snap and button clothes, uses pop-lock beads and locking blocks with some assistance. Practices with playdough scissors, perhaps using two hands to open and close the scissors. May practice using one hand with a child-safe screwdriver. | With increasing interest and ability, manipulates objects. For example, pulls a chain to turn on a light and opens doors, latches, or zippers. May also squeeze water out of sponges and other water toys. Scissor accuracy is increasing. For example, may use one hand to cut and one hand to hold the paper. Turns toy screws by hand or with a tool. | With less support from adults, is able to manipulate objects with fingers. For example, can pull locking blocks apart or roll playdough into small, compact balls. Can cut along lines or make a desired shape or outcome with small tools. For example, can fit the nail into the hole and hit it with the hammer. |
| PM2.2 Dexterity: Uses fingers to manipulate objects. | Pincer grasp improves. For example, frequently grasps puzzle pieces and places some easily. Shows interest and some skill (with support) in holding large crayons or other writing tools. Depending on finger strength and awareness, the lines drawn may be light. Finger and brush painting may be deliberate. For example, a child may make a swirl of green mixed with blue to represent a lake. | Uses large crayons, markers, and painting tools to support increased accuracy with intended shapes and drawing. Is more accurate with placement of objects. For example, can use the large tweezer in the science center to pick up different objects of interest. | Child is able to add detail to drawings. May make a more detailed self-portrait, for example, with lines for hair, half circles for ears, and more. Shows increased dexterity with small tools like writing utensils, tweezers, or scissors. |

**Anti-Bias Learning Experiences**
Create positive social identities by encouraging passing/sharing games with small objects. Encourage children to practice tying, buckling, or snapping their shoes or clothes. Encourage others to help "teach" how to tie. For example, draw a diagram with children that shows how to tie a knot. Offer a variety of fine-motor activities, such as beading, sewing, building, and mixing.

## Standard three: Healthy and Safe Living Practices

Standard three includes both understanding and practicing health and safety behaviors. Teachers can help children build competency in this area by leading conversations about healthy foods, describing ways we can prevent illness, emphasizing the importance of rest, and teaching students how to wash their hands, wipe their noses, or help clean tables.

It might seem as though there is little room for variation in safety and health practices because they are "just common sense." We urge teachers to remember that common sense is only common when people have the same experience. Therefore, as children learn the basic health and safety practices, teachers can keep in mind that understanding health and safety practices are personal experiences first. If, for example, children do not practice frequent handwashing at home, it may be a challenge to instill this as a common practice in the classroom. Teachers can stay aware of their personal bias when it comes to health and safety practices to avoid judgmental messages. There are different cultural expectations and practices about personal care and hygiene. It is a teacher's job to uncover her own bias and practices in order to be supportive of others' practices.

For example, most would agree that healthy food is essential—but perspectives on what is "healthy" vary widely. For example, a vegetarian teacher would want to be careful to provide a balanced perspective about what "healthy" food is. It would be inappropriate to say, "I don't eat meat because it's not healthy" when children are being offered meat as a protein component in their meal. It would be supportive to say, "I didn't choose meat for my protein today. You have [food name] today." Or, "I didn't grow up [eating meat] in my family. What does your family like to eat at home?" Teachers must also remember that images in the greater community portray opinions about health. For example, some families may eat fast food on a regular basis, while others never eat out at all. A child who experiences one, the other, or anything in between can be taught, "Schools have rules we follow for children's health and safety, and families have their different ways of doing things. Some people in our room or our community do [this] and others might do [that]. The most important thing is that we are all safe and healthy."

Students demonstrate growth in their awareness of health and safety in many ways. Emergent learners might remind their friends to wash hands before lunch. A child who is not used to holding hands may struggle to walk with a group when going to the park and need extra attention to stay safe.

As understanding grows, children may more frequently cover their coughs, wash their hands, and blow their noses independently to demonstrate that they understand and can be responsible for appropriate health and safety tasks. Children will also identify which tools and tasks are reserved for adults. They will be able to explain why and make intentional efforts to be safe. They can demonstrate how they avoid things that could cause injury. A child at this stage might point to the bottle of table cleaner and say, "That's just for grown-ups to use."

Children can also show proficiency in healthy behaviors when they begin to understand and accept limitations around much-loved activities and treats like computer time and candy. They know sunscreen can prevent sunburn and looking both ways helps you cross streets carefully. A child at this stage might tell everyone at circle time that seatbelts "save lives." Proficient children may share what they know verbally or in actions. It is important to remember that health and safety norms can be learned. Teachers can keep this in mind when a child is new to the room and watch for signs of growth in understanding as the child becomes accustomed to new surroundings.

## STANDARD THREE: HEALTHY AND SAFE LIVING PRACTICES

| Skill | Emerging | Developing | Proficiency |
|---|---|---|---|
| PM3.1 Self-care: Shows awareness of body care routines. | The child shows interest in self-care practices such as with hair, body, and teeth. Practices with the tool for each. | Practices self-care routines with assistance. May try to snap barrettes into hair, for example. May notify others that she washed her hands and now they are very clean. | With greater accuracy, expresses interest and acts with intent to care for self. For example, may try to "brush every tooth" or remembers to wash hands after coughing or sneezing. |
| PM3.2 Bodily protection: Shows awareness of physical safety. | With some support and assistance can talk about safety plans and rules. For example, thinks about putting a coat on to "protect me from the cold." | Communicates certain activities as off-limits to children. For example, pauses to ask if she can take a turn on the climber. | Helps remind others to be safe. For example, may pretend to "buckle up" when going for a pretend drive. Or may remind others to "be careful" when hauling sand from one end of the play area to the other. |

### Anti-Bias Learning Experiences
Make posters for younger children to remind them to wash their hands. They can build confidence by showing off their self-help skills through making documentation boards or helping make a classroom daily schedule poster.

Compare classroom routines to family life. Parents can contribute stories about what their routines were like when they were little. Make books about different family health routines for children to explore.

## Standards and Domains: Using a Balanced Perspective

When we understand learning standards, we do not leave the success of our classrooms to chance. Setting realistic expectations for our students helps us individualize our attention, a principal goal in anti-bias teaching. We can also use our knowledge of learning standards to connect social and emotional development with anti-bias thoughts and actions.

Earlier, we mentioned how some parents have difficulty connecting with educational programs because of the negative experiences they may have had in school. Teachers are shaped by early academic experiences too. Some of us loved language arts and science. Others might have excelled in math. It is important that we plan for and teach each domain with equal enthusiasm, time, and resources, regardless of where we have felt most competent in the past.

If we feel intimidated by a domain, we can find professional development support and commit to being a co-learner with our students. For example, teachers who do not like to sing or think they are "bad" singers can sing along with musical supports such as radio stations or albums to ensure their own biases about music do not limit children's exposure to music. Using music regularly and consistently gives children dancing and singing time, and their bodies and brains benefit from it as well. Gradually, teachers should sing more freely as their confidence grows and as the children learn to sing along too.

In chapter 6, Anti-Bias Observation and Assessment, we describe how teachers can construct a lesson plan that sees and attends to the full developmental picture of each student. The chapter details how we can enact these lesson plans while incorporating anti-bias principles, self-reflective work, domains, standards, and child input.

## Chapter Point Summary

1. Programs must connect domains and standards with their own state's quality requirements.
2. Learning standards help us set and maintain developmentally appropriate learning expectations for our students.
3. Teachers can set and implement anti-bias goals in each learning domain.
4. Teachers must give equal consideration to each domain, regardless of our preferences. If we need to increase our competency in a particular area, we can seek out professional development opportunities.

 Scan the QR code or visit www.redleafpress.org/abc /sd.pdf to download or view the YWCA Minneapolis Early Childhood Education Anti-Bias Preschool Curriculum Domains and Standards.

# CHAPTER SIX

# Anti-Bias Observation and Assessment

## *How do I use observation and assessment to support children?*

Through anti-bias observation and assessment, we can connect children's play to learning domains and standards. When we adopt an ongoing, authentic assessment practice, especially one that is grounded in a philosophy of equity, our instruction can change to meet children's learning needs. We believe in a teaching paradigm that fuses curriculum, instruction, and engaged, authentic assessment. (See Jardine 2017 for information on the topic of reevaluating teaching practices.) The YWCA Minneapolis anti-bias curriculum is in line with the National Association for the Education of Young Children (NAEYC) and National Association of Early Childhood Specialists in State Departments of Education (NAECS/SDE) joint position statement on Early Childhood Curriculum, Assessment, and Program Evaluation (2003). We believe successful anti-bias assessment requires teachers to observe children's choices and use them to assess, scaffold, reflect, and support growth.

Observing and assessing children helps teachers decide how, when, and where to teach. This is an extremely powerful position. (See Gibbons 2011 for more about the ethical and existential ramifications of teacher perceptions.) We think as anti-bias teachers it is our job to make sure that we are clear about our motives and perspectives. These are limited by our experience—a self-reflective practice can help us see how. The American Psychological Association (2012) reported "self-revealing interaction" (56) as a powerful strategy to overcome prejudice. We take this to mean that not only do we need to look deeply into ourselves, but we also need a community in which to share. It is important to remember with this practice, as we have said before, that it is not anyone else's job to help white people unpack their racial bias. Each is personally responsible. When a group shares a common goal of reflection, "unpacking" becomes a common goal of the group. The APA reported that working toward cooperation in groups is also an effective way to challenge negative bias. What these two examples tell us is that anti-bias work is not limited to siloes; when working as a team, teachers can plan for observation and assessments that are anti-bias in nature. Anti-bias practitioners use observations and assessments to make sure we use a balanced perspective as we teach and evaluate our students.

The following are four main reasons we observe and assess:

1. To meet the individual needs of the children
2. To teach to the group's zone of proximal development

3. To support families and community
4. To learn about our own teaching and grow professionally

As we have discussed, the early learning domains, standards, and terminologies used across the country echo each other. Since we share a common framework for setting developmental goals and expectations, programs can use a variety of tools to observe, document, and assess growth. Some common assessment systems are the Work Sampling System and the Classroom Assessment Scoring System.

We do not believe that there is one correct way to measure learning. At the YWCA Minneapolis, we use a mix of documentation tools alongside our own observation and assessment structure. This structure ensures that observations are gathered and evaluated within an anti-bias framework.

The YWCA observation and assessment system was developed to do the following:

- support our mission, vision, and values
- show evidence of learning during play
- explain the benefits of early childhood education
- show parents how their children are developing
- show stakeholders how children are learning in our environment
- validate what we do as early educators
- document stages and growth

The principles that guide the curriculum also define the way teachers observe and assess children. We believe this work should help us

- treat families as partners;
- recognize that children learn through play;
- take children's and parents' thoughts, ideas, and feelings seriously; and
- individualize our teaching.

This structure can be used in addition to whatever tools you have adopted for observation and assessment. It will help you strengthen your anti-bias practice.

## Authentic Observation and Assessment

The adjective *authentic* means "original, true, and factual." Authentic observation to us means real and honest. Real and honest also means anti-bias, because unnoticed assumptions and prejudices can block or cloud vision. At the YWCA, we also believe that authentic observations and assessments are ongoing and that they should analyze children in real-life experiences, from playtime to pickup time. An ongoing structure means one or two children are observed and assessed daily in a rotation; not all children are assessed every day. Ongoing observation and assessment structures help teachers

- decide which experiences to offer;
- know which materials to bring into the classroom; and
- know when to scaffold learning.

When we practice a routine system of observation and assessment, we set ourselves up for success. We can be more sensitive to the needs and interests of our students and use what we learn to shape our weekly lessons. Our planning can also be responsive to input from families.

When we use ongoing observation and documentation, we are more prepared to communicate with parents. Reports and data are readily available. We can show evidence of growth through our notes, pictures, and the collected work of students. Conference preparation is done ahead of time, as teachers have steadily gathered detailed assessment information in each child's portfolio.

This method can also support the overall health of your organization. Directors can measure center-wide performance when classrooms collect and share information about learning and readiness. They can use the data from ongoing daily assessments and observations to plan for future programing.

Susanne Denham, Hideko Bassett, and Susanne Miller (2017) researched factors that contribute to ECE teacher stress and possible departure from the field. Not surprisingly, higher stress is linked with poorer classroom interactions. One factor that makes it difficult for teachers to have more joyful and stress-free interactions is lack of control, including the scheduling of daily activities. Teachers are often frustrated about the many add-ons that have found their way into the classroom. In our research, we have found that many teachers have assumed that assessment and observation of children was a task to be done outside of the classroom, privately and away from children. Additionally, we have found many teachers worry that they will not have the time to commit to an ongoing observation and assessment system. We have found, however, that once teachers have established a routine system, daily assessments become a cornerstone of teaching rather than another burdensome, squeezed-in chore. We believe that more enjoyable and natural interactions between teachers and children will occur when teachers have more time to do what they love—teaching children.

Without an organized system, we can forget to write down our observations. Instead of planning, we might wing it, using a general sense we have of each child and broad kindergarten readiness goals rather than scientifically based learning standards for preschoolers as our guide. We are often unprepared when we need to show documentation of a child's progress. We may end up backtracking, trying to remember and record what a student did yesterday or last week. This leaves room for unintentional bias to take root and distort our evaluations.

Teachers need to be present with children during playtime to authentically observe, record, and assess their learning. Playtime should be varied and have minimal interruptions. Teachers should limit taking children out of their play to perform tests, and they should also avoid setting up "have-to" activities ("everyone *has* to practice writing at this table today") that force children into showing their skills. When "have-to" activities lead the programming, they pull children away from what really engages them. In addition, required activities trap teachers in one place, removing them from many opportunities for shared experiences and educational conversations with children about their work.

Authentic observation happens when children are being themselves and their play is self-directed. We often say, "A moving child is a learning child." It is our job to embed the early learning standards into the life of the classroom, so that any activity can give us information about a child's progress through each learning domain. We can also add a question or enhance an activity to guide our observations. For example, if a child is focused on block building, the prepared teacher can observe language and literacy growth by encouraging her to create a sign or explain her thinking. We can set the stage for authentic assessment. Children at play are happy and engaged. Engaged children are willing to be challenged a bit more in their learning. Engaged children provide unending authentic information about their development.

One of the benefits of an authentic observation and assessment structure is that it helps us achieve an anti-bias educational goal by encouraging our children to develop positive self-images. Play is the work of children; it is how children learn, thrive, and develop who they are. When we engage in observations, we show them that we respect their work. Students begin to recognize their abilities. They see and talk about the learning process. They toot their own horns! A child who experiences ongoing, authentic assessment might say, "Teacher, you need to write this in my folder!" and "Teacher, look what I can do! I couldn't do that before." Children can truly be learning partners with their teachers.

Our classrooms are busy. Our work is complex. That is why we believe it is important to develop an observation and assessment system that is a routine part of the day. Next, we describe how we structure ongoing and authentic observation and assessment in YWCA classrooms.

## The YWCA Minneapolis Anti-Bias Curriculum Assessment and Observation Structure

Each teacher makes time to conduct two authentic observations on two children each day. It is important that collections are scheduled and routine so teachers stay on track. Observations can happen during any activity, including these:

- pretend play
- mealtimes
- transitions
- small groups
- large-muscle time
- creative art experiences
- outdoor play

# Observation and assessment schedule

This table shows a possible schedule for individual observations for each child in every domain on an ongoing basis. With twenty children and two teachers, the cycle completes every seven weeks. You can make your own schedule using your teaching team and children in your room. Some teachers find it effective to divide children into consistent groups in which one teacher is primarily responsible for their core group. In some settings, all teachers, assistant teachers, and aides will take notes during the day. The teacher responsible for the group will compile the collected notes at the end of the week. Teachers must be aware of the variety of standards within domains to avoid neglecting parts of the skills needed to develop full proficiency. We believe that teachers together should share their observations and ideas to support growth and development. We also think children can be included in this process.

| OBSERVATION AND ASSESSMENT SCHEDULE | | | | | | | |
|---|---|---|---|---|---|---|---|
| Week | Domain | Teachers | Monday | Tuesday | Wednesday | Thursday | Friday |
| Week One | Social and Emotional Development | Teach. 1 | Child 1 & 2 | Child 3 & 4 | Child 5 & 6 | Child 7 & 8 | Child 9 & 10 |
| | | Teach. 2 | Child 11 & 12 | Child 13 & 14 | Child 15 & 16 | Child 17 & 18 | Child 19 & 20 |
| Week Two | Approaches to Learning | Teach. 1 | Child 1 & 2 | Child 3 & 4 | Child 5 & 6 | Child 7 & 8 | Child 9 & 10 |
| | | Teach. 2 | Child 11 & 12 | Child 13 & 14 | Child 15 & 16 | Child 17 & 18 | Child 19 & 20 |
| Week Three | Language and Literacy | Teach. 1 | Child 1 & 2 | Child 3 & 4 | Child 5 & 6 | Child 7 & 8 | Child 9 & 10 |
| | | Teach. 2 | Child 11 & 12 | Child 13 & 14 | Child 15 & 16 | Child 17 & 18 | Child 19 & 20 |
| Week Four | Creativity and the Arts | Teach. 1 | Child 1 & 2 | Child 3 & 4 | Child 5 & 6 | Child 7 & 8 | Child 9 & 10 |
| | | Teach. 2 | Child 11 & 12 | Child 13 & 14 | Child 15 & 16 | Child 17 & 18 | Child 19 & 20 |
| Week Five | Mathematical Development | Teach. 1 | Child 1 & 2 | Child 3 & 4 | Child 5 & 6 | Child 7 & 8 | Child 9 & 10 |
| | | Teach. 2 | Child 11 & 12 | Child 13 & 14 | Child 15 & 16 | Child 17 & 18 | Child 19 & 20 |

| Week Six | Scientific Thinking | Teach. 1 | Child 1 & 2 | Child 3 & 4 | Child 5 & 6 | Child 7 & 8 | Child 9 & 10 |
|---|---|---|---|---|---|---|---|
| | | Teach. 2 | Child 11 & 12 | Child 13 & 14 | Child 15 & 16 | Child 17 & 18 | Child 19 & 20 |
| Week Seven | Physical and Motor Development | Teach. 1 | Child 1 & 2 | Child 3 & 4 | Child 5 & 6 | Child 7 & 8 | Child 9 & 10 |
| | | Teach. 2 | Child 11 & 12 | Child 13 & 14 | Child 15 & 16 | Child 17 & 18 | Child 19 & 20 |

## Sample observation and assessment documentation tool

This example shows what documentation can look like when observations and assessment are ongoing and authentic.

| FIGURE 2. | | | |
|---|---|---|---|
| **Domain** | **Watch for/Standards** | **Child's Name: Derek** | **E/D/P** |
| Social and Emotional Development Date: 6/4/20 Date: 7/16/20 | Emotional Security | *6/4 Stated feeling "giant happy" in circle time. Talking about going to park with family yesterday.* | D |
| | Self-awareness | | |
| | Community, People, & Relationships | *7/16 Exclaimed, "I'm a reader!" wide stance, fisted raised hand.* | P |
| | Social Understandings & Relationships | | |
| Approaches to Learning Date: 7/16/20 Date:_____ | Inventiveness, Problem Solving, and Curiosity | *7/16 Eyes on work while holding conversation in kitchen/shopping.* | E |
| | Interest & Persistence | | |
| | Processing and Utilizing Information | | |
| Language & Literacy Date: 7/16/20 Date:_____ | Listening, Understanding, Communicating, & Speaking | *7/16 Said "Donut is for me, Derek. Doctor Derek gets a Donut. D, D, D." Sound and name practice. Makes up his own L word play.* | D |
| | Emergent Reading Skills | | |
| | Emergent Writing Skills | | |
| | Computer Knowledge | | |
| Creativity & the Arts Date:_____ Date:_____ | Exploring & Expression | | |
| | Music & Movement | | |
| | Dramatic Play | | |
| Mathematical Development Date:_____ Date:_____ | Numerals & Patterns | | |
| | Measurement | | |
| | Geometry, Spatial Thinking, & Data Analysis | | |

The examples offered in Figure 2 were gathered by a teacher at the YWCA. The following is a description of the scene that offered the opportunity for authentic observation.

It was the second week in the assessment cycle, and teachers focused on growth in the Approaches to Learning domain. Ms. Trinh had glanced at the files of the children who were on her list to observe today. Since her observation cycle repeated every seven weeks, Ms. Trinh had several cycles of assessments for each child. She had a good idea of where everyone was at in the Approaches to Learning standard.

Ms. Trinh could also see the evidence of growth that she had gathered last week to track social and emotional development. For example, she had a photo of "toy washing for the store" in Derek's file. She had noted that he stayed focused and shared ideas for play with friends during the activity. When she connected these observations with learning standards, she could see and show his emerging emotional security and self-awareness. Ms. Trinh was excited to share this data with his parents at their next conference.

At 10:00 a.m., Ms. Trinh entered the kitchen area where a few children were busy collecting, cooking, and sharing play food from the shelves. The documentation tool on the top of Ms. Trinh's clipboard had her notes from last week regarding social and emotional development.

The children knew it was Derek, Nina, Sam, and Kaylee's turns for observation and assessment. Ms. Trinh kept a calendar with the children's names in the circle area. It was part of the daily schedule to announce whose turn it was to have the teacher take special note of their work. This routine made the children very aware of what Ms. Trinh was up to. They had become experts in the process and liked showing off their learning.

Ms. Trinh smiled at the group and said, "Derek, last week you helped make a plan for the toy store and washed the toys for a long time. Do you remember that?" He did. All the children in the kitchen today had something exciting to share about their participation.

In this conversation Ms. Trinh said, "I know you all have such great memories. Derek, would you please explain to me what you are playing here today? I'll make notes."

"I'm shopping," said Derek. He was dressed in a doctor's coat and wearing plastic heeled shoes with an open toe.

"Oh, I see," Ms. Trinh said. "What are you shopping for?" Ms. Trinh had been practicing her self-awareness over the last year and noticed she did not like that this boy was wearing "girl" shoes. She noticed the thought, let it pass, and continued with giving her attention to the group and Derek in particular.

Derek continued his work as he answered. The fact that Derek talked to her while still continuing to take food off the shelf and place it in his bag told her he was gaining in standard one—Inventiveness, Problem Solving, and Curiosity in the Approaches to Learning domain. He was also progressing in standard two—Interest and Persistence. She wanted to collect some data for the Language and Literacy domain and continued her interaction.

"Can you tell me about what you are doing here, Derek?"

"I'm getting food for my patients," Derek replied.

"That's what I thought," Ms. Trinh answered. "I wonder, do you need a list?"

Derek paused a moment and then said, "Yes!" There was paper and a pencil on a clipboard nearby. Ms. Trinh reached for it and asked Derek to tell her what he needed. She drew symbolic pictures for the items. When Derek was ready, he came to see his "doctor's list."

"Can you tell me what this donut starts with?" Ms. Trinh asked.

"Donut is for me, Derek!" he said.

"You are right, Derek. It is also the first letter in *doctor*. Doctor Derek gets a donut!" she said and asked, "What letter is that?" and made the *D* sound.

Derek laughed, repeated the little phrase, and said "*D*!"

Ms. Trinh made an extra note to show evidence for growth within the Language and Literacy domain. She documented that Derek was making progress in standard two—Emergent Reading Skills. Ms. Trinh was also able to collect data on his physical and motor development. His manipulation of the pencil showed her that his fine-motor skills (standard two) were developing. Ms. Trinh had been watching his fine-motor development closely because his parents had asked specifically about it in conferences a month ago. She liked to give them frequent updates on his progress.

Ms. Trinh decided to ask Derek what other letters he knew even though it was an Approaches to Learning day. He seemed very interested in letters, sounds, and the "doctor list," so she wanted to see where this investigation would take them.

"What else do you have on this list?" she asked.

Derek pointed to the lemon on the list. "This is also for me!"

"How is the lemon for you?" Ms. Trinh smiled as she asked.

"My last name. La, La, Lagos! An L!" said Derek.

Ms. Trinh gave him a high five. "You are a reader!" she said.

"I'm a reader!" Derek echoed. "I'm a reader" was a phrase Ms. Trinh used with all the children to support each of their efforts in reading. The path to reading is filled with many stops along the way, and each child was in a different place. She used this phrase to affirm where the child was at the time and used it to build confidence. What confidence indeed! Derek's stance was wide and his hand shot up in a fist as he repeated the common and affirming phrase. Ms. Trinh made another note to show Derek's progress in Social and Emotional standard two—Emotional Security.

In this example, Ms. Trinh engaged Derek in an "educational conversation" where they both participated in a reflective learning process. Educational conversations contain a series of feedback loops between teacher and child. Each takes a turn leading. Educational conversations have two goals:

1. To gather information about skill development
2. To teach something new about that skill

The educational conversation Ms. Trinh had with Derek was an essential part of her engaged observation. Without the conversation, it would have been just an observation. It was within the educational conversation that Ms. Trinh conducted her assessment and instruction.

In a scenario like this, a teacher will likely be interacting with other children simultaneously. Conducting a planned observation and assessment of one child does not mean input from other children is discouraged. A skilled teacher will create space for each child to speak and share knowledge. A teacher may even choose to make additional notes about children not on the observation schedule—that is definitely fine! The point is that each child is authentically observed and assessed in a structure that works to support authentic, play-based learning.

This example is just one of many possible ways an ongoing, authentic, play-based assessment could go. All teachers need to develop a system that works for their style.

## The Process of the Observation and Assessment

Not only does each teacher need to develop a practice of observing and assessing, but each must also strive to understand every child at each point of development. It is a complex process of differentiation in which individual differences are supported in all domains, standards, and stages of development. To keep this process from becoming too overwhelming, teachers can break the process up by making time for weekly and daily planning. Here are the steps we follow when we observe, document, and assess learning:

1. At the end of the day, during naptime, or first thing in the morning—whenever you are not in the classroom supervising children—review the evidence of learning in a child's portfolio to consider the child's current level of development on a particular skill.
2. Make plans to observe for the domain and the standard next in order. Consider where the child was in this domain and standard when last observed, keeping in mind that it could be quite a while in the past. If you have data for the domain standard from previous observations, you can more thoughtfully decide what skill can be supported today.

3. During a play-based observation and assessment, collect information as "data": a short anecdotal note, a sample of the child's work, or pictures. Add this evidence to the child's portfolio.

4. Consider the data and draw a conclusion about the child's level of development in this domain standard and skill. This is a return to step one—consider the child's current level of development.

As you can see, preparation is a key component to capturing those special, authentic moments that tell us so much about where our students are and where they are preparing to go.

## Giving Extra Attention to Social and Emotional Progress

Brandon Becker, Kathleen Gallagher, and Robert Whitaker (2017) focused their research on teacher well-being. They firmly believe that the emotional and social disposition of children and teachers are intricately related. We agree that the complex ways in which teachers view the children in their care are colored by the vantage of their personal experiences and professional development. Assessing a child's development will then be affected by a teacher's past and present experiences.

Here is an example of how one teacher, Ms. Keena, noticed her personal and professional experiences having an impact on how she assessed a child's stage of growth and development. Ms. Keena describes herself as growing up in a predominantly white community, and the images of people she saw on television and other media sources were of the white dominant narrative. "I've always understood that self-awareness and commitment to eliminating racism was a lifelong journey," she said, "but I guess I was not aware how deep my bias runs. I never stop being surprised. I am willing to take time to look. There is always more about myself that I can learn. I understand we all have individual experiences, and that leads to us each feeling differently about ourselves and the children we take care of. But it is only though a great effort on my part that I tune into the very subtle ways I think and feel. Doing this makes me more comfortable that I am viewing children's development as equally complex stories. I have to be aware of who I am to really be close to knowing others."

We think that the greater the extent to which teachers are aware of their personal experiences and are able to connect knowledge of them to teaching and expectations, the better informed they can be when assessing children's development. Teachers' levels of social and emotional development help them build relationships with children. We also think the value of mindfulness cannot be overstated. Mindfulness can also lead to a calmer state of mind that can make managing a roomful of young children go more smoothly.

The YWCA believes when we are assessing for another domain, we must always pay attention to social and emotional development. Social skills development and emotional maturity are integral to success in life. A child's emotional management skills lay a foundation for all other learning. For example, speaking one's mind is essential for children to communicate their needs. Children who can say, "I want the green paint" are sharing their needs in social situations and negotiating the use of materials. They are building cognitive, creative, and fine-motor skills.

Often, social and emotional learning opportunities catch us off guard. The only way to scaffold and teach a new social or emotional behavior is within real-life situations. That is why it is essential to have authentic, up-to-date documentation about social and emotional development to guide our instruction. These assessments are particularly useful when we communicate with families, especially when either parents or teachers have concerns about progress.

## "Now What?" A Guiding Question

After evaluating progress and reaching a conclusion, the teacher must ask, "Now what?" Say the child has mastered a standard. The teacher could ask, "Now what should my future plans for the child be in this area? Should I help the child act as a peer tutor for others? Should I enrich the classroom with additional opportunities that move the child even further in development?"

Or, let's say the child is only beginning to develop in the standard. The teacher could ask, "So what will I do to scaffold growth to the next level? What might I do during our lunchtime conversations to help this skill emerge? What could we do outdoors? What activities could I add to an area the children are enjoying right now to further develop these skills?"

When teachers use assessments to inform their instruction, the "Now what?" question is crucial. Teachers must not forget this question when they close the portfolio and put it away until the next time. The "Now what?" question is what keeps the cycle moving. "Now what?" is when teachers like Ms. Petra say, "I love thinking about other things we can do to move forward."

As Ms. Petra also shared, "It is so much fun for me to make this room a constant work in progress where everyone is learning." Ms. Petra's positive mindset is crucial; a teacher's answer and attitude toward this question provide another hypothesis upon which to conduct an experiment, collect more data, develop another conclusion, and ask again, "Now what?"

The YWCA anti-bias observation and assessment formula looks like this: teacher understanding + shared activities of the child's choice + engaged observation + scaffolding of learning + documentation of growth + self-reflection and celebration of growth = intentional teaching and authentic assessments.

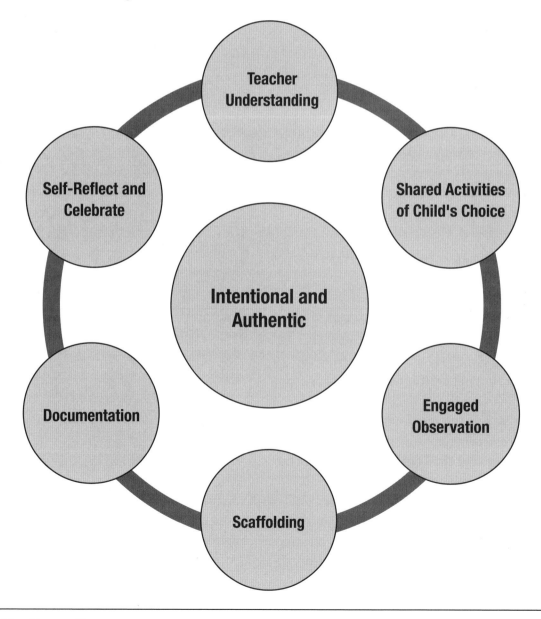

Did you notice that celebration is part of the formula? A key purpose of daily, engaged, authentic assessment is to demonstrate to all the children in the classroom that it is a place where learning is important and valued. Don't be shy. Tell children how great they are! Show you care, and be obvious about your observations. We might hear teachers say, "I write down what you do because I care about helping you learn," or "I am here to write about what a learner you are." Celebration is an essential part of the process. During observations, we should find an aspect of growth to reflect on and celebrate. We can ask, "Remember last week when this was kind of hard for you?" and then recognize growth by saying, "And now you can do it!" Our actions match our words when children see us write their accomplishments down and hear us share their triumphs with their families.

Here is an example of a time when a new item on the menu threw some children for a loop and set the stage for ongoing assessment of social and emotional development, scientific thinking, and math. Sweet red peppers were served as the vegetable. The children in Ms. Lucie's room were not sure about the bright red raw vegetable on their plates. Most didn't eat it, and the teachers were frustrated with the many complaints. She asked the children what they knew about peppers. Chatter filled the classroom lunch tables with the children's responses:

"They are icky!"

"We use them at home."

"I don't like them!"

Ms. Lucie decided to try a strategy she called "lucky day" with the recalcitrant group. She explained that these peppers were sweet and had more vitamin C than an orange. "Now, let's see who's having a lucky day," she said to the class. All the children's ears perked up at that. Their lucky day? A child asked what that meant. "It means if you like the taste of this sweet red pepper you will be happy. If you are happy, you will be lucky. Let's smell this pepper together. What do you smell?" A couple children seated at the table near Lucie lifted the pepper suspiciously to their noses and sniffed. "I smell peppers," said one. "I smell sweet," said another. "Let's taste it. You can just lick it if you are still wondering," Ms. Lucie said. Some nibbled, some sniffed, and some just tasted with their tongues. "Who's lucky?" Ms. Lucie asked the group cheerfully. "I am!" said one, and

Lucie clapped, offered a high five, and from there started cheering for each person who was lucky. Those who were not so "lucky" were patted on the back or hugged and told by their teacher, "It's okay. You will maybe be lucky next time." Ms. Lucie said she loved this strategy because "I think lunchtime should be happy, and I want children to know they are not either 'good' or 'bad' for how they choose or don't choose to try something new. If someone likes it, good for them, and if not, good for them for trying, and maybe next time they will like it better. My class has come to love this strategy too. We keep a Lucky Day chart in our room. Now, anytime someone tries something—and it doesn't have to be just food—they can put an X by their name." Through the lucky day strategy, Ms. Lucie was able to observe several different domains for several children.

Every day is different in a preschool classroom. Some days you might not have an opportunity to assess two children. Life happens. But we are confident that once you put this assessment system in place, you will be more likely to practice it on a regular basis—even on the busiest days.

## Chapter Point Summary

1. Anti-bias observation and assessment connect children's play to the learning domains and standards.
2. Observations and assessments coupled with a self-reflective practice help us develop balanced perspectives.
3. Programs can use a variety of tools to observe, document, and assess growth.
4. An ongoing structure means children are observed and assessed daily.
5. An authentic observation and documentation system helps us give parents accurate, up-to-date information.
6. Teachers need to be present with children during playtime to authentically observe, record, and assess their learning. This approach encourages healthy self-images, an anti-bias goal.
7. Preparation is key.

## CHAPTER SEVEN

# The Anti-Bias Classroom: Lesson Planning, Teaching, and the Learning Environment

*How can anti-bias teaching strategies support optimal play-based learning?*

It is common today to talk about "living" or "working" documents. When people use a living document, they plan for it to grow and change. We think of our curriculum in this way too. It has the children's lives built into it. Our lives and the lives of families shape curriculum. So how can we create a curriculum that best supports play-based learning?

The YWCA Minneapolis anti-bias curriculum is founded on the principle that learning happens through every experience a child has, and we believe learning is optimized through play. When teachers use a daily structure that is play-based, children feel safe to express and explore their own ideas and perceptions of the world. Since we strive to affirm our students as individuals, as parts of their families, and as directors of their learning, play-based learning is a foundational aspect of the anti-bias classroom and our curriculum.

As we have said before, we acknowledge this topic is deep and varied. Early childhood education has such a rich history of play and learning theories and studies to draw on. In this chapter, rather than assess data and research, we explain how anti-bias teachers listen to children, follow their interests, and consider their individualized goals and needs in order to plan lessons. In this chapter we describe how our teachers use this process to create play-based learning experiences that guide development, we share their methods and stories, and we demonstrate how room setup can inspire high-quality play and support anti-bias teaching.

## Play-Based Learning

Everywhere, every day, children are playing. Some say play is the number one unifying action of people in the world—play is serious stuff. Michael Yogman and colleagues (2018) stated that play is not thoughtless. We think play is the work of the child. In one of our teacher development sessions, we ask teachers to share an activity they loved to do when they were children. Answers ranged from quiet alone time to group and free-play time, to adult- or older peer–guided play. Some memories are fond, and some carry sorrow. After sharing the memories, teachers are asked to think about how they felt when it was time to stop playing. They are asked to remember what their bodies felt like when they had to switch gears, come in, sit, listen, or wait. We are not advocating that children never "stop" playing but rather are asking teachers to recognize the sense of peace and joy they found when doing something that brought them pleasure or what it was like to yearn for it. Play is the lifeline of a child. It is at play that they can feel free, and with freedom comes learning. When teachers understand it is the natural inclination of a child to wish to engage in interesting and fun activities, we can embed learning opportunities into extended periods of play. We have all seen what happens when children do not feel they have had enough freedom to be creative and explore—they do it anyway and cause disruption to the room, or they withdraw and don't seem to progress in learning. With this knowledge in mind, children's caregivers should always prioritize play. Play offers healthy development that is not just physical. When children play, they are also developing socially, emotionally, and cognitively. Play builds skills across all domains, giving children opportunities to build their self-esteem and lower stress.

Many of us worry our preschoolers will not be ready for kindergarten unless we coerce their cognitive development. We assume that children are learning only if they are sitting still, reciting numbers in a row, or playing quietly. This is a very dangerous assumption. Adults may feel more comfortable learning this way, but children do not. When we look at the world through a child's point of view, we can see why.

We think children at play see their world with all the lights on—while adults see the world with a flashlight. Alison Gopnik (2012) explained that young children in play are clever and thoughtful scientists. We take this to mean that children do not naturally focus on one thing as many adults do. Children at play can test their ideas, try new things, and make mistakes freely. They are seekers, questioners, wonderers, and wanderers.

Children naturally play, but they are not born knowing how to get the most out of their play. That is where we step in. With our guidance, children can develop their social systems, cognitive skills, and capacity for executive functioning. We can foster high-quality play by incorporating the following in our curriculum:

- activities that extend over hours or days
- problem solving
- make-believe
- invisible or handmade props
- role playing

As we stated in chapter 5, it is our job to follow our students' playful interests and to enrich those choices with conversations, activities, and materials that move them through the learning domains. Here is how YWCA teacher Ms. Cadee used play to drive learning.

Keona and Marselle were sitting together talking by the window. Ms. Cadee stepped closer to listen. The girls were switching back and forth between being a parent who was dropping children off before she went to work, to being a grandparent who would watch the children, to being the child.

"Can I be the grandparent?" Ms. Cadee asked.

Keona and Marselle smiled. "Yes," they said.

"Say goodbye to your mom, girls. We are going to have fun today!" Ms. Cadee said.

"Bye, Mom," the girls said. They waved.

"What do you want to play today?" Ms. Cadee asked, still pretending to be their grandparent.

"Let's play magic," said Keona. Soon the girls were making a play story about a magical land where they were in charge.

Keona and Marselle continued the play story for days. Whenever Ms. Cadee asked them what was happening in their story, they added more.

"We had so much fun," Ms. Cadee recalled. "There were hidden magical items we were finding, the children made maps, and I was able to get great assessments and observations that showcased their skills."

This kind of teaching may appear to be completely spontaneous, but it is not. It takes planning and a skillful application of developmentally appropriate, anti-bias practices. Remember, NAEYC tells us we must lead rather than follow the development of children. We use what we know about students' prior skill levels to lead their development through each learning domain. We also connect children's questions and curiosity to anti-bias principles. Doing this, we believe, builds an open and respectful learning culture.

Teachers guide learning by listening to children. All teachers should be familiar with the learning domains and use their knowledge to have units, concepts, and projects planned before they teach. The YWCA curriculum organizes its lesson plans around the following twelve themes:

1. Animals and Insects
2. Fall
3. Winter
4. Spring
5. Summer
6. All about Me and My Family
7. Healthy Living
8. Five Senses
9. Earth and Environment
10. Safety
11. Motion and Movement
12. Community around Us

Planned themes give teachers and children a jumping-off point for play. They also help visitors and families understand and visualize play-based learning. The themes are intentionally broad and will not limit child-directed play. The teachers and children craft the lesson plans weekly. These plans grow to accommodate the thoughts, hopes, and needs from children and families.

Teachers guide children's play by providing the necessary tools and equipment. For example, typical block areas contain a variety of building materials of various sizes and shapes. They may also offer a variety of dolls, community symbols like schools or parks, or vehicles. This is not the only way anti-bias teachers guide play. We listen to children's stories and observe their skills. We make sure our block areas reflect their lives and interests, capture their stories, and scaffold their development in the most supportive and positive ways possible. Here is what block area play looked like in one anti-bias classroom.

Ms. Anna observed the children playing and noticed that they were very interested in the road construction happening outside the building. The children loved to watch the diggers and the cranes moving sections of concrete off the street. They watched in wonder as the workers dug holes and laid pipe under the street. They asked questions about what was happening.

Ms. Anna filled the block area with tools to mimic the behavior the children were seeing just outside their window. She sat with them, guided their conversations, and reminded them of what they observed while watching the workers. Ms. Anna engaged the children in role play and, using conversational questions, encouraged them to explore dilemmas and solve structural problems. She created a safe space for the children to explore and question what they saw, heard, and knew. She found that each domain and standard of learning could be engaged as she followed their interest in construction.

Modifying curriculum to add focused play experiences—in this case, incorporating the construction outside the window—is fairly common in our classrooms. According to Ms. Petra, another YWCA teacher, "I try to notice if there are any trends in my children's learning and behavior. I use the information for my planning. I can assess every domain and standard. . . . It's easier to do because they are having fun and I know the standards."

We know that if children are happy in their play, we will get more accurate information about their learning. When teachers make decisions about what to offer in play, they know which of those skills to embed in that play in order to scaffold the children's learning. From there they can assess children's current skill level.

## Anti-Bias Teaching Strategies

When teachers make plans that directly relate to the interests of the group, they recognize and respect the importance of culture in children's lives. This approach takes into account children's families, home lives, and languages, as well as their perspectives and understanding of their world.

### Impromptu experiences lead to long-term discovery

Anti-bias teachers must be aware of how the outside world can affect the students in our class. In the following example, an experience with a book that contained gender bias inspired Ms. Dianne to better connect her students' home lives with their preschool lives.

The theme for the month was "All about Me and My Family," and Ms. Dianne had planned to read the story *The Family Book* by Todd Parr during circle time. When Jada brought a book from home, however, Ms. Dianne decided to switch gears. Jada told the class that she and her family read this story together. Here was a chance to share a real-life family tradition!

The book features a father who stays home with his young child because the mother is sick. The dad makes every mistake imaginable, from burning breakfast to ruining the laundry. In the end, the child saves the day by ordering pizza after Dad creates a fiery fiasco at dinnertime. The story is full of gender stereotypes, but Jada was excited to share something she and her family loved with her classmates, so Ms. Dianne read the book to the group.

After sharing the story, Ms. Dianne had two goals. She wanted to honor the child who brought the book, but she also wanted to be sensitive to the other children and respect their experiences of family. Reina, for example, lived with her uncle and had a grandfather who was a great cook. Ms. Dianne wanted to make sure Reina and the rest of her students felt respected and acknowledged.

"Besides not letting the gender bias go unchecked, I mostly wanted them to notice that families come in all sorts of ways, and each one is correct," said Ms. Dianne. "The main thing is the love and caring each person gives in their family."

After the story, Ms. Dianne encouraged the group to talk about how their families differed from the one in the book. She did this by asking the open-ended question, "Are all dads bad cooks?" What followed was a lively conversation about who can cook, what happens in a home, and favorite foods. Dianne made a note to bring in more books to illustrate how equally competent and capable mothers and fathers can be and to recognize families with adopted children. Later, she went online and looked for books that addressed gender bias.

Ms. Dianne said she became more interested in gender bias as a result of this experience. "I found there was a lot to learn about how we are taught about men, boys, women, and girls through these everyday stories. It is almost invisible, but it's totally visible at the same time. I decided to introduce a version of the 'I Am From' poem we teachers did as part of our self-reflective practice to my class."

Here's how she changed the questions to engage her young learners:

1. What does your family say to you?
2. What do you love to play the most?
3. What special places do you like to go to?
4. What else do you know?

The answers to the questions were attached to the following four beginnings:

1. I am from my (mom, dad, and family member) saying . . .
2. I am from playing . . .
3. I am from going to . . .
4. I am from knowing . . .

Here are two samples of finished poems:

*I am from my mom saying, "I love you!"*
*I am from playing at the park and swimming with my dad.*
*I am from going to my cousin's house.*
*I am from knowing everyone is doing everything, and the sun is orbiting the earth.*
*—Aria, age four*

*I am from my mom and dad. They say goodnight to me.*
*I am from playing with my hat and trains.*
*I am from going to watch the trains.*
*I am from knowing my mom is coming today.*
*—Cyrus, age four*

Ms. Dianne's story illustrates how teachers can turn an unexpected classroom moment into a meaningful lesson. In an effort to address gender bias, Ms. Dianne slightly modified an activity and reminded her students of their individuality. The table below shows how Ms. Dianne incorporated children's interest and themes to drive her lesson planning.

| THEME: ALL ABOUT ME AND MY FAMILY | | | | | |
|---|---|---|---|---|---|
| Learning Domain | Monday | Tuesday | Wednesday | Thursday | Friday |
| Social and Emotional Development | What is a family? | Family story sharing | What is special about your family? | My friend's family | Classroom job changes |
| Approaches to Learning | Poem planning session | Ways of folding paper | Planning project display | Update the dramatic play area | Final book work |
| Language and Literacy | Read previous poems | Labeling images | Computer printing | Poem books | Display share |
| Creativity and the Arts | Decorating our books | Bear family snack | Duckling craft | My special song | Family "crest" |
| Mathematical Development | Likes and dislikes chart | Page numbering | Shape stickers | Magazine cutting and gluing books | Shape stamps |
| Scientific Thinking | Magazine gluing, placement | Book progress sharing | Paper airplanes | Family trees | Food choices page |
| Physical and Motor Development | Toy washing | *Make Way for Ducklings* (McCloskey) | Simon Says | Sing "The Bear Went Over the Mountain" | Basketball |

The class worked on their "I Am From" poems for a week. On Monday, they started making their lists. On Tuesday, they wrote their poems. On Wednesday, they glued their poems onto colored paper. Then they decorated the paper with paint, wooden sticks, shapes cut out of tissue paper, and photocopied and printed pictures of themselves. (Children could choose whether they wanted to use a family photo or an individual photo.) On Thursday and Friday, children shared their work with the class during large-group time. The following Monday, Ms. Dianne hung the poems up in the hall for families to read.

Ms. Dianne added documentation of child learning in the display as well. She included photos titled "Social-Emotional Development" with captions that read, "Children thought about self, families, and favorite things. This builds skills in naming preferences and helps children understand that each person has a special and different family."

She titled an image of children decorating their frames "Creativity & the Arts, Fine-Motor Skills, and Math" with the caption, "Children used open-ended materials to show feelings, develop one-to-one correspondence, and practice hand-eye coordination."

A third photo set showed children sharing their work with the class during large-group time. Ms. Dianne labeled this, "Language & Literacy and Science." The caption said, "Practicing talking about our work. Asking and answering questions builds our listening, communication, and scientific-thinking skills."

Because Ms. Dianne used authentic assessments and strong relationships with families to get to know her children, she was able to be culturally responsive *and* standards-driven in her approach. She used the "I Am From" poem to support development in multiple domains. The following list shows how domain connections were made:

## Social and Emotional Development

- Children described their emotions.
- Children sustained attention and persisted.
- Children described themselves and their families and family traditions.

## Approaches to Learning

- Children invented personal ways to fold paper.
- Children continued work throughout the week with goal in mind.
- Children shared ideas for display.

## Language and Literacy

- Children listened during circle time.
- Children wrote their poems.
- Children shared their poems with friends.

## Creativity and the Arts

- Children used a variety of art materials.
- Children used different media to express thoughts and emotions.

## Mathematical Development

- Children counted the lines of their poems.
- Children talked about time spent on poems.
- Children used shapes and shape vocabulary in design.

## Scientific Thinking

- Children discussed sight, sound, smell, taste, and touch in individual poems.

*Physical and Motor Development*

- Children developed fine-motor skills through writing.

You will notice that the sample lesson plan from Ms. Dianne's class mostly highlights learning experiences that would best be enacted during circle time and free-play time, but these are not the only places learning happens. Our days are packed with anti-bias teaching opportunities. Welcomes and goodbyes, meals, and toileting are all routine moments that offer teachers the chance to build relationships and practice skills. The plan is just a guide the teacher uses to make sure ample opportunities to support children's growth and development are given on a daily and weekly basis. Use this checklist to evaluate your teaching strategies:

- ☐ Teachers see family as the core of a young child's learning and development.
- ☐ Teachers ground child development in relationships.
- ☐ Teachers allow children's emotions to drive early learning and development.
- ☐ Teachers respond to children's self-initiated exploration.
- ☐ Teaching is individualized.
- ☐ Teachers honor family culture and home languages.
- ☐ Teachers are intentional.
- ☐ Teachers plan for and expect change. They create opportunities to talk about diversity.
- ☐ Programs create time for reflection and planning.

## Families at the center of learning

YWCA teacher Ms. Ashley knows that as an anti-bias teacher, she should make families the center of her students' development. She makes time every day to sing a song about family. Here is how the song would go for a child named Sarah:

*Sarah has a mom and her name is Desiree.*
*Sarah has a mom and her name is Desiree.*
*Sarah has a mom and her name is Desiree.*
*Oh, she loves Sarah so!*

"A young child sees the world through her relationships," explained Ms. Ashley. "She sees who she is when we sing this song. After we sing, we each take a turn to share something about the person we sang about. How a child expresses their thoughts and feelings are individual. One child may add a bit to the song, another may clap, yet another may speak or laugh. It is the teacher's role to recognize and affirm children. It's not always easy. Sometimes they say something that is hard. Then we have to talk about our thoughts and emotions."

Ms. Ashley modifies the song as needed to accurately reflect each child's life. "We know that a stressed brain can't think, so it's important that we navigate through tough times as calmly as possible. In this case, I wait for children to initiate who they want to talk about. This gives a consistent space to talk about, reflect, and recognize all the people who love them. Because I know this, I can be very thoughtful when I do this song with the group. It's very emotional sometimes, for all of us."

Each time she sings one of these songs, Ms. Ashley is celebrating the children's unique upbringing while also allowing them to build a variety of skills. Diversity comes in all aspects of our identities. As Ms. Ashley shared with another teacher, "There is diversity everywhere. We have diversity of confidence levels, race, ethnicity, culture, family structure, and so on. Another student is practicing waiting her turn and listening. This song gives us time to talk about important things on their minds and practice skills that need attention every day."

How did Ms. Ashley do on the checklist? Let us take a look.

**Teachers see family as the core of a young child's learning and development.** Family is the main focus of the family song.

**Teachers ground child development in relationships.** The song is about relationships, which inform learning.

**Teachers allow children's emotions to drive early learning and development.** Choosing whom to sing about and what to say supports emotional development that will also drive learning.

**Teachers respond to children's self-initiated exploration.** The teacher is responsive to individual choices and responds to child-initiated communication.

**Teaching is individualized.** Even though the children are in a group, this song offers an individualized experience by allowing them to create their own songs.

**Teachers honor family culture and home languages.** The teacher knows the family culture (family history) and can incorporate home languages.

**Teachers are intentional.** The teacher has already taken time to observe the children in her class, allowing her to be intentional with each child.

**Teachers plan for and expect change. They create opportunities to talk about diversity.** Allowing each child to choose whom they want to sing about and to share their unique story is an example of planning for diversity.

**Programs create time for reflection and planning.** The teacher knows that the song can inspire a variety of emotions, and some are difficult to process. She makes time for reflection and plans how she can further support her class.

Ms. Ashley uses a flexible and responsive approach in her lesson planning as well. Here is an example of how she transformed a planned theme to reengage student interest.

The theme was "Motion and Movement," and when Ms. Ashley heard her children discussing how fast they could run in their shoes, she was excited to follow their lead. In the next day's morning meeting, Ms. Ashley wrote on the easel: "I can _____ in my shoes." Children took turns practicing writing things like "run," "jump," "race," and "play." Ms. Ashley and her teaching team had planned to organize study around clothing later that year. They decided the time was ripe to explore this subject!

Ms. Ashley set up a shoe store in the pretend play area and spent many hours encouraging play, supporting play, and observing and assessing children's development. The children measured their feet, wrote orders for shoes, counted out money for purchases, and made signs for shoe sales. Children practiced roles such as shopper, store clerk, and stock worker. They even made paper slippers.

After a few weeks, the children were slowly losing interest in the shoe store. Ms. Ashley paid attention to their conversations to see what they were thinking. Were there events happening in the community or at home that could be connected to classroom learning? She checked in with parents and discovered that many families were excited for the Summer Olympics to begin.

"What do we know about the Summer Olympics?" Ms. Ashley asked during circle time. The children were excited to share what they knew and what they wondered about the games. "I heard from your families that some of you know a little bit about the Olympics. I wonder, would it be a good time to change our play area from the shoe store to an Olympic Games site?" Ms. Ashley said. The class was very interested. They made a list of all the ideas they had for the play area.

At free time, the class started packing up the shoe store and building the game site. The children were very talkative; they asked questions and swapped facts about athletes and their favorite sports.

The group decided that the indoor site would include flags, medals, and indoor versions of the long jump, high jump, and a beanbag shot put. They set up track, Frisbee, and tennis events outside. As a special treat, teachers showed short clips of people running in races, performing gymnastics, and competing in swimming. Ms. Ashley brought in real-life athletes too, including a YWCA staff member who came and spoke to the class about her experience as a team swim coach. Further inspired by their interest, Ms. Ashley also taught her class about the Special Olympics. She told them about these separate but equally important games for children and adults with physical and mental disabilities. To the play area, the class added braces from the disability unit to mimic a physical disability, wore a blindfold to model vision impairment, and wore headphones to experience deafness.

Ms. Ashley connected the following learning concepts to Summer Olympic play:

*Social and Emotional Development*

- Children talked about whether they got faster or slower each time and why these differences came about.

*Approaches to Learning*

- Children showed interest in developing a new play area.

*Language and Literacy*

- Children created personal scorecards and flag designs.

*Creativity and the Arts*

- Children made personal anthems.

*Physical and Motor Development*

- Children engaged leg, torso, and arm muscles in sports.

*Mathematical Development*

- Time: children used a stopwatch to write and recognize numbers, understand time, and measure how long it took to run a lap.
- Measurement: children measured jumps with a ruler and their weight with a scale.

*Science*

- Children questioned the phenomenological aspects of movement.

The Olympics was not a topic Ms. Ashley had planned for when she developed the shoe store, but as the shoe store became less of an interest and the games grew in popularity, it was an easy transition to make. Ms. Ashley actively engaged in child conversations and acknowledged their contributions by tuning in to their questions. She was able to facilitate engaging, relevant play because she listened to children's and family's ideas and took them seriously.

Ms. Ashley's story shows us how much more effective we can be when we focus on child-directed conversations. Children show us what we need to do next. Children's questions and passionate conversations are invitations to adults to slow down, speed up, explore something new, or change tracks all together. They also give us the opportunity to drive language learning. Jennifer Whorrall and Sonia Cabell (2016) stated that teachers can respond using open-ended questions to build essential preliteracy skills.

Helpful phrases teachers can use to capture children's ideas include the following:

- Let's talk about it!
- Let's write that down and talk about it next week.
- Tell me more about that!
- What else do you know?

Ms. Dianne describes what this process looks like for her: "When my kids say they want to go to the moon, I don't say, 'No, let's go somewhere we can really get to' or 'You can't,' I say, 'How can we get there?' 'What will you do?' 'What will be the best thing about it?' 'What will we need to bring?' and so on." A conversation for children is often not about getting to a final end point. They do not want to actually *get* to the moon; they want to *play* at getting there.

# Invitations for learning and following children's lead

Children's invitations come in the form of their questions and ideas. These questions and ideas then provide an opportunity for engaged learning and, when we are familiar with domains and standards, we receive unexpected opportunities to conduct authentic observations and assessments.

When YWCA teacher Mr. Kai was derailed from a planned observation, he was able to find out valuable information about a student and encourage development toward another standard. Here's his story.

Mr. Kai was sitting with several preschoolers at the writing table during small-group time. "Oh Javon, you have an orange crayon and an orange shirt," he said. "Can you show me where the orange letter is?" Mr. Kai motioned to the colored letter cards in front of Javon.

Javon pointed to the *J*. It was not orange. "Mr. Kai, this is a J—that starts my name!" he said.

Although Mr. Kai's goal that day was to assess color recognition, he noticed that Javon recognized the letter *J* as the first letter of his name. He took this as an invitation to explore letter recognition. He responded to this invitation by continuing with the rest of Javon's name.

"It sure does start your name!" he said. "Can you find the next letter in your name? Can you find the *A*?"

Javon found the *A* and proceeded without prompting to find the rest of the letters in his name as well. Mr. Kai saw Javon's interest in spelling his first name as an invitation to move him along further toward recognizing and spelling his whole name. He found an *M* and asked Javon what his last name was.

"My last name is Moore, Mr. Kai," Javon said. Mr. Kai pointed to the *M* and asked him if he could identify the letter.

"*M* like in *mommy*!" Javon replied.

"That's right, Javon, *M* is for *mommy* and for your last name: *Moore*."

Javon took the *M* and put it next to the letters that spelled out his first name. Together, he and Mr. Kai found a couple more *M*s and talked about the sound the *M* makes. They talked about other words that started with *M* too—like *mouse* and *mitten*. Mr. Kai knew that the next time he wrote Javon's name, he would add the *M* for Moore.

Mr. Kai's goal had been to use the letter cards to assess color recognition, but because he was willing to accept Javon's invitation, Mr. Kai collected valuable assessment information about how far Javon had come in learning the letters of his name, and they got the chance to celebrate that accomplishment! Mr. Kai will be able to assess and focus on color recognition at a different time. Encouraging Javon where he was most engaged is more important than adhering to a strict assessment schedule. When we follow children's interest, we are really encouraging the development of Approaches to Learning, which supports all learning now and in the future.

Opportunities like this one occur every day. When teachers respond and revise their plans, they demonstrate their respect for children. They are also able to delve deeper into a topic, bring back an activity from the previous week, or take a side trip from their plans for the day or the week.

## Let's take a trip

Teachers and children are always on a learning adventure. The learning standards are our destinations, and the curriculum is the route. Play, of course, is the transportation. We map the route to individualized learning goals using lesson plans, the children's interests, the children's lives and cultures, and our shared classroom experience.

Sometimes the teacher plans the trip. For example, intentional teachers know they can help children practice a variety of skills while they develop a make-believe restaurant. In one example, children were creating a restaurant because Mai See's uncle just opened a pho restaurant, and Mai See was excited about it. Mai See's teacher, Mr. Isaac, recognized this excitement as an invitation to pursue a new dramatic play center. He even invited Mai See's uncle to visit the classroom. Mai See's teacher understood how to embed each domain and standard into the planning and play, and he knew how to provide support while helping children lead the project.

Sometimes, teachers accept children's invitations for a side trip. Suppose that in your science area, you have set out several books about chickens and their life cycle. You have also set up an incubator with fertilized chicken eggs.

You have ensured that your art center is ready for all sorts of chicken art by providing art supplies that engage the children and encourage creativity. Empty boxes are ready for the children to decorate and prepare with bedding to serve as baby chick houses.

In the science center, you have displayed how-to pictures that show the steps of making a waterer for the chicks and the steps of preparing chick food. You have provided a twenty-one-day timeline with photos of the developing chicks.

In the home living area, you have set up a pretend farmyard and have provided plenty of materials for dress-up and pretend play. You already know that this month-long project will address all domains and standards.

You begin the unit.

Almost immediately, you take a side trip.

A child asks, "Are these eggs like the kind we eat?" This question makes you realize your children think of eggs in terms of food, not animals. You had not thought about cooking with eggs or tasting different egg dishes. The child's question invites you to add to your plans, and you accept the invitation.

"Yes, these eggs are like the kind we eat. They look the same, but a rooster fertilized these eggs, and baby chicks are inside growing," you answer. "I'll bring in other eggs tomorrow—eggs we can eat. We will talk about what to cook with them." You add this side trip to your plans. At group time, you tally the list of the children's favorite egg dishes.

"Teacher," says another child after a few days of study, "look at my picture of a chick! I need some feathers to glue on it."

"We have art feathers in the red bin," you answer. "What colors do you think we need for your pictures of the chicks?" When the feathers are used, you and the children find ways to represent feathers with other materials you already have on hand, and in no time you've learned how to make feathers from construction paper.

A child exclaims, "I want to take home a chick after it hatches!" This one takes you by surprise. You have to think it through.

"I think we need to talk about this tomorrow. We will see how many children are interested, and then we'll decide what to do next." The child recognizes the respect you have shown and feels encouraged and heard.

You make a note to revise your large-group plan for tomorrow. You decide to talk about farms and farming. You also decide to send letters home to see how many families have the desire to adopt baby chicks. You wonder how many families have—or are willing to get—a permit from the city to keep backyard chickens. You think perhaps this could be a great home-school connection. You also think of inviting families who do keep backyard chickens to come to your classroom and talk about raising chickens.

If you have planned for flexibility, each question or comment from children can take you on an exciting side trip. Planned flexibility opens up many opportunities that might otherwise be overlooked. How? You have already planned your unit. You already know which learning standards your unit addresses. You have decided on learning activities that help you move children closer to accomplishing those learning standards. With your attention to children's questions and conversations, all you change is the route you take toward your goals.

Teachers who are willing to add to, remove from, or extend a unit due to children's questions and comments are practicing responsive teaching. This kind of teaching does not do away with preplanning several units of study. It does, however, add a new layer of preparation—being prepared to revise your teaching while you are teaching. When teachers accept children's invitations, they create better learning environments.

We must also look for, expect, and plan anti-bias teaching opportunities. When teaching about chicks, for example, you could ask the following questions:

- Who can be a farmer?
- What kinds of smells are on a farm?
- Do all people eat chicken?
- What do you eat at home?
- Are there parts of the world where there are no chickens?

Teachers can choose any unit or project to use as long as they remember to plan for flexibility. When they do, they ensure that each and every day the children, powered by play, are slowly moving toward a final destination: growth and achievement.

## Families help plan learning

As we discussed earlier, children bring their home culture into the classroom with them. We can be intentional about building stronger bonds with parents by inviting families into our classrooms and including them in our lesson planning.

A healthy teacher-family partnership sends the message to children that their families and teachers are working together and that they can feel safe with their teachers. Positive teacher-family relationships provide a connection between home and school and help children feel comfortable in the classroom. YWCA teacher Mr. Rob looked for signs that he was building those positive relationships. He hoped children would want to give him "a high five every morning . . . just to know they feel at home, safe, and loved." This kind of comfort is the result of a strong relationship between teachers and families.

Mr. Russell, another teacher at the YWCA, included a child's family in the classroom's learning experiences. Here is his story.

Amy had been excited for weeks because her grandmother was coming all the way from Nigeria to visit her. Amy did not know how far away Nigeria was, but her parents and her teacher, Mr. Russell, kept telling her it was very far.

Amy could hardly contain her excitement on the day her grandmother was due to arrive. When Amy came to school, all she could talk about was her grandmother. She was finally here! Mr. Russell and the class decided to invite Amy's grandmother to her classroom.

In preparation for incorporating Amy's grandmother's visit into the weekly plan, Mr. Russell had reached out to Amy's mother. "Amy has been so excited about her grandmother visiting," he said. "I am wondering if we can invite her to spend some of the day with Amy here at school. Do you think she would want to come?"

"I think she would just love that!" said Amy's mom. "I will talk about it with her when we get home."

Amy's grandmother was very happy about the invitation. She planned a day and time with Mr. Russell. On that day, Amy proudly brought her grandmother into the classroom, showed her around the room, and introduced her to her classmates.

Amy's grandmother asked Mr. Russell if she could tell the children one of the stories she told her children and grandchildren. Mr. Russell told her he would love that, and so would the children. The story was about animals and their friendship and how they overcame a problem.

Amy's grandmother was animated and joyful as she told the story. She even sang during parts of the story and involved the children by teaching them to chant what the animals said. All the children had fun and thoroughly enjoyed the story.

After the story, Mr. Russell encouraged the children to draw a picture of their favorite animal they had heard about in the story. Amy's grandmother drew a picture too.

According to Whorrall and Cabell (2016), the conversations that children have come from their experiences. The invitations you receive from them will always connect to the lives they live, the places they call home, and the special people in their lives. When we respond to children's invitations, we connect to their families.

## Practices that foster flexibility in the classroom

These key practices foster anti-bias teaching and support flexibility:

1. Listen carefully.
2. Use humor.
3. Be a role model.
4. Be consistent.

**Listen carefully.** Listening is as important for teachers as it is for children. It is easy to hear children's voices but not actually *listen* to what they are telling us. If you listen carefully and with intention, children will tell you what they need.

Listening to children lets them know that you are interested in who they are and what they think. This responsive teaching, in turn, supports the healthy self-image and self-esteem that are necessary for learning self-control and positive social skills. Here are some strategies for careful listening:

- In conversation, use "I heard you say" to check for understanding. For example, "I heard you say you don't think it's fair that Justin gets five more minutes on the swing. Is that right? Yes? Can you tell me more about that?"
- Refrain from analyzing the child's story or feelings.
- If you noticed a trigger, use self-reflection to get to the bottom of it. If you are caught up in the net of your unconsciousness, it is impossible to support the child's needs.
- Breathe slowly, slow down, look the child in the eyes, and hold the child's hands to indicate your mental and physical presence with the child.

When teachers listen attentively, they help children develop emotional intelligence.

**Use humor.** Humor can go a long way with preschoolers. It is effective at breaking tension, avoiding a struggle, and reminding children of rules and limits. It also shows your human side. Children love to laugh, so fill your classroom with laughter!

In one of our centers, a preschool room was working with papier mâché. The class was clamoring around the sensory table. The table held bins with a glue-flour mixture and newspaper strips. There were balloons and paintbrushes. One child sniffed the glue mixture; another poked at it with her finger.

Ms. Diana explained that some people use papier mâché shapes to make their self-portrait. She started to sing, "I'm gonna try this. I'm gonna try this. Watch me go." She used a brush to stick the paper onto a balloon with the liquid starch and glue mixture. "Ooh, it's ooey, ooh its gooey." Soon kids were singing, trying, and enjoying the novel experience.

**Be a role model.** The most effective way to teach children positive social behavior is to model it. Our generosity, attentive listening, respectful treatment, and intentional inclusion of children's questions and comments will greatly benefit the development of children's social skills. You can model

- the rules of polite conversation;
- how to name feelings;
- being adventurous;
- problem solving;
- using tools and equipment;
- safety behaviors; and
- self-help skills.

And so much more! Teachers should model everything we want to see happen in our classrooms. When we model behaviors, we encourage children to practice these skills too.

**Be consistent.** Your consistent attention, intentional listening, joyful interactions, and willingness to accept children's questions and ideas all contribute to an anti-bias classroom. Taking all children's ideas and feelings seriously supports equity.

In summary, anti-bias teachers accept verbal and nonverbal invitations from children. They look for and create opportunities to talk about diversity. Anti-bias teachers include families, keep play as the focus, look to support children emotionally, meet the needs of individuals and the group, and stay flexible. Being flexible for the children in your classroom can mean opting to change the dramatic play area or noticing that high levels of activity in the room call for an impromptu outdoor walk. Play-based learning environments help children develop their skills in every domain and every standard.

## Environments

Teachers can design their environments to promote positive peer-to-peer and adult-to-child interactions. If the learning environment is not responsive to children's individual needs, interests, and strengths, they can become restless and bored. We think one of the best ways to achieve a cooperative, caring, and harmonious atmosphere among young children is to meet children's basic social, emotional, physical, and cognitive needs. Offering authentic, manageable, stimulating, and challenging learning experiences within an organized, attractive, and safe environment addresses these basic needs.

Play is the mechanism through which children move and learn, so everything we offer young children must be done with this fundamental mindset first and foremost. Erica Danniels and Angela Pyle (2018) helped define the current state of play-based learning. One thing they reported is that there is tension between child- and adult-directed play. We think a balance of both is appropriate. The environment can be set so that children have room to make their own stories, games, and adventures. It can also be a place where teachers can engage to support and direct learning using both anti-bias principles and the learning standards their curriculum is set to meet.

Environments that are otherwise carefully designed and equipped for young children may not meet the needs of children with disabilities. We must adapt our environments carefully and intentionally for any children with physical challenges, learning disabilities, or emotional needs. Here are some simple accommodations that make our rooms more inclusive:

- Use large lettering.
- Incorporate sign language.
- Reduce distractions, glare, and overstimulation.
- Use visual schedules.

This is not an inclusive list by any means. We also have found that these kinds of thoughtful adaptations are helpful for many of us without any diagnosis. We rely on community supports for children with diagnosed needs. We encourage you to connect with local agencies that offer support for individual children in your care.

## Design your learning environment

No two learning environments are the same in design, shape, size, layout, or location. The equipment and materials vary and are specific to each program. A preschool learning environment must be carefully, thoughtfully, and intentionally planned and designed. We know that the physical setting of a classroom has a great impact on children. It must promote children's learning by offering an interesting, attractive, and comfortable setting. The space must be also be organized to meet a diverse set of children's needs as well as to offer a sufficient number and variety of developmentally and culturally appropriate materials and equipment.

When we are intentional about the room's design and layout, we can find a variety of ways to teach equity and fairness through the everyday experiences in our room and make our room welcoming to all. We think it is more than just photos on the wall showing a variety of skin tones, cultures, and ethnicities in a variety of roles. These things are very important, but it is also important to have representations of the children, teachers, families, and community at large in our rooms. For example, baby dolls with varying skin tones; dolls that are culturally representative, such as Kachinas, Matryoshkas, corn husk dolls, peg wooden dolls, rag dolls, etc.; and a variety of props and clothing allow children to explore many of the roles they witness in their daily lives outside of the center. This helps to make a learning environment anti-bias.

It has been our experience that racism and other discrimination makes people uncomfortable. For example, have you ever been in a room where all the baby dolls were white? Or a room where boys are discouraged from playing dolls or cooking? Did you notice these messages? Did you feel comfortable or uncomfortable? Being aware of how you think and feel about race and gender expression (and other types of human differences) can help you be intentional with the children in your care. These seemingly simple yet profound educational experiences can, when used intentionally, help teachers teach anti-bias messages in their rooms.

Safety should always be a priority as you plan your classroom layout. Think about each area and the type of safe play activities that can happen there. A poorly organized layout can create problem areas. These include spaces that encourage wandering, running, or unsafe behavior as well as pathways that lead nowhere or interfere with play already in progress.

Early childhood environments should be rich in experience, play, teaching, and people. Children need to explore, experiment, and learn basic knowledge through direct experience. They need agreed-upon limits and rules.

Children seek out a constant change of stimuli. The more time children spend in a learning environment, the more variation and stimulation they need. Plan your environment to include a variety of dimensions, such as closed, open, soft, hard, high, and low. Plan for large-group and small-group areas. Provide spaces for quiet and active experiences. The environment should support large- and small-motor experiences, movement, social experiences, sensory learning experiences, cognitive experiences, problem solving, and language and literacy experiences.

## Layout

The layout of your classroom frames the learning experiences offered there. It guides how the space will be used. To design your learning environment layout, think of the room as an empty space. Consider the look and feel of the room from a child's perspective. Get down on the floor, look around, and ask yourself what will be going on in the classroom. Think about the rhythm, movement, and flow of the day. Think, too, about how children and adults will interact within the layout.

Your fixed spaces (walls, windows, doors, bathroom, closets, and so on) will shape your learning environment layout. Floor coverings can determine the location of learning centers. For example, carpets that provide cushioning for little bodies and absorb noise are suitable for quiet areas. The furniture, equipment, and materials used for learning centers and for storage, adult spaces, and shelving require thoughtful placement and should also be considered in the layout.

As you plan the physical layout of the classroom, think about boundaries for specific learning centers. Boundaries can be physical (such as a curtain or shelf), or they can be symbolic (such as a taped area or a stop sign). The boundaries of learning centers should allow children to move comfortably, using their whole bodies, around and within the classroom. You can make boundaries within your classroom using furniture, room dividers, or changes in the floor surfaces. Almost anything can serve as a divider, so long as it is safe: shelves, furniture, fabric hung from a line, streamers attached to the ceiling, folding screens, or even puppet stages.

Every element in the classroom influences how it feels in your setting. The lighting, the colors, the textures, the noise level, what is on the walls, and even what is *not* in the room—all make a difference in how children will interact with the space, with one another, and with you. Experiment with these elements of the environment to find the best mix for the children who spend time there. For example, say fighting often occurs in the block center. Perhaps your furniture arrangement has created too small a space in that center. You could enlarge the center and observe the play. If children are still having social difficulties in this center, perhaps you could add more materials—especially more of the favorite items—to create peaceful play.

The flow of traffic within the environment can either prevent or cause problems. Young children fit and move through spaces differently than adults. When a learning environment is well organized, with open pathways that clearly lead to engaging activities, children can manage on their own. When the flow of traffic is carefully planned, children can move freely from one activity to another, allowing teachers to attend to individual children according to their needs. The layout should accommodate the physical needs of children with special needs, as well as any assistive technology used by them. Flexible environment layouts are important for children who use assistive equipment, such as a wheelchair. The layout will direct the traffic and influence the flow of activity within your learning environment. Consider the following questions as you design your layout:

- How does traffic flow in the environment?
- What are the busy areas, and where should they be located?
- Where do children seem to congregate?
- Where do routine daily activities take place?
- Are personal belongings easily accessible for all children?
- Do children have easy access to learning materials?
- Are the learning centers defined?

## Learning Centers

A well-planned environment contains a variety of defined areas where children and adults find materials that suggest a particular type of learning experience. These learning centers allow children to follow their interests and provide them with hands-on opportunities. Learning centers communicate to preschoolers which activities can occur in that spot.

Plan and design learning centers carefully to support learning projects. Centers should have materials that can be used in multiple ways to support the development of specific skills. You can set up learning centers to facilitate either teacher-directed or child-directed learning experiences while supporting standards and learning objectives and furthering anti-bias objectives. For example, can your "kitchen" area have images from local restaurants or clean and recycled food boxes from families' homes? Do you have photos of families around the room, or pictures of the local bus stops, post offices, or other public places like schools, libraries, or restaurants that family and community members might frequent? Can the science center include local found objects like branches, shells, rocks or other interesting items?

Ms. Mila wanted to make her room more inviting to the families, who represented many different countries of origin. She asked the families about their child's favorite items or places in their homes, and they shared many answers when she brought this subject up at pickup time. Mila decided to pay a visit to a local shopping center. There she found inexpensive wall hangings that warmed up the look of her room's walls. In a thrift store she found a variety of picture frames. "The children and I put photos of their home life in the new frames on the walls," she said. "They have stayed interested in this for a long time now. I think we are going to make a framing shop in our dramatic play area next."

The centers help shape your classroom layout. Arrange learning centers in your classroom in a way that accommodates the character of each center. Each center requires a particular size, shape, location, and contents. The literacy learning center, for example, should offer children a comfortable, soft, quiet space to read. The art learning center should allow preschoolers to be messy as they create artwork. The block learning center tends to be noisy and may be a common conflict area.

Be creative and follow the children's lead to design your learning centers, but remember to double-check your state's standards as well as any additional accreditation and licensing organizations you report to before going full steam ahead. The following list outlines typical learning centers in early childhood programs:

- dramatic play center
- block center
- art center
- music center
- manipulatives center
- library center
- science center
- computer center
- sensory play center
- large-muscle center

## Tools, Equipment, and Materials

Tools, equipment, and materials are resources for adults to use in teaching and reinforcing learning as well as for children to enjoy through play. Most programs need to have specific equipment, materials, and toys to comply with state or local licensing requirements. Carefully selected, developmentally appropriate materials give children opportunities to practice newly acquired skills and to understand the concepts they are exposed to through the curriculum.

Some materials are suitable for child-directed activities, while others need teacher supervision and direction. Learning materials can be simple, complex, or super complex. Simple materials are those with essentially one function. Complex materials are those with two functions. Super-complex materials have three or more functions. Children need to experience all of these levels of complexity in learning materials.

To inspire children's imagination and creativity, provide open-ended materials they can use in a variety of ways. Fill the learning environment with materials that support sensory experiences. Offer opportunities for children to explore light, color, sound, and motion. Include materials in the environment that help preschoolers discover many textures, shapes, and sizes.

Sprinkle the environment with surprises and treasures that energize children. For instance, imagine the look on a preschooler's face upon finding a music box in a hidden place. Think about a variety of materials that invite learning, including natural items, recycled items, and objects from home that families share with the classroom. Remember, teacher-made materials are just as effective for children's learning as commercially made materials and toys. Teacher-made materials can be designed to support specific learning goals and learning activities.

Adults want to be around things that they like, that they identify with, and that make them comfortable. This is true of preschoolers too. The materials and equipment in your classroom should be things preschoolers like, identify with, and feel comfortable around. Here is what one YWCA teacher did to make sure her classroom contained cultural touchstones that would help her students feel more at home.

As she planned materials for each of her learning centers, Ms. Terry kept the families' home lives and parents' jobs in mind. She asked families to bring empty food boxes from home, which she then covered with clear contact paper and put in the dramatic play area. She thought about which costumes and props to offer the children for dress-up. Eddie's father was a firefighter, so Ms. Terry made sure she had items in the dramatic play area for firefighters. Not only would Eddie be proud of having things that reminded him of his father, but the other children would also enjoy playing with them.

She was also very intentional when planning the classroom library. Ms. Terry included books that told stories about friendship and how to get along with others, books whose characters lived in the city and in apartment buildings, and books that reflected different family structures. She thought about the children who had pets at home and included books about children and their pets. It was fun for her to think about the children's home lives and find books that reflected these lives.

Ms. Terry asked families to bring in pictures of themselves. She copied these pictures and displayed them throughout the classroom on shelves and blocks. She also made sure that there were several shades of skin colors for all of the materials in the art area. The children could see and use skin colors not only like their own but also like those of their classmates. Because Ms. Terry believed it was important that she carefully and intentionally considered what was in her classroom. She tried to provide family and home-life connections within each learning center.

## Choices

The preschool learning environment should be set up to offer children a manageable number of choices. Children should be able to select the materials and toys they want to use or play with. Over time, preschoolers become increasingly competent in making choices. Children need to have some choices but not too many. Too many choices can be overwhelming.

Learning materials should be rotated periodically to expand children's experiences and play. Reintroducing familiar materials and toys can also inspire new ways for children to use them. As you watch how children respond to the environment and hear the ideas that emerge from their play, you can offer them additional materials to expand their learning. One YWCA teacher used these parameters to design a space that would support high-quality teaching and learning.

Mr. Andre stood in the doorway and surveyed his new preschool classroom. It was a large room, with a sink and storage cabinets on the far wall. There was a bathroom in the corner. He liked the big windows.

Mr. Andre knew his first priority was to keep his children safe. He evaluated areas where children might climb, run off, pinch fingers, open windows, and hide. He noted spots where spilled liquid might create slipping hazards. Were there any maintenance issues he needed to address? He looked for peeling paint and signs of pests and insect infestations and noted any unlocked teacher cabinets and closets.

As Mr. Andre walked into his classroom, he knew he had to consider many things as he planned the physical design of the room. He asked himself,

- How do I want my preschoolers to feel during the time they spend in this room?

- What messages do I want parents to receive when they come into the room?
- How can I support play through the learning centers and their placement?

In his notebook, he sketched out the floor plan of the classroom, contemplating the paths children would take to move through the room and get to the learning centers. He added sketches showing where he might place the furniture. He contemplated colors, lighting, and how to use the shelves to divide the space. To his delight, the large windows offered lots of natural light. Sitting down in one of the preschool-size chairs, he surveyed the room from the children's view. He reminded himself that his preschoolers' perspective of the room would be different from his own.

Mr. Andre knew he had a lot of work to do to get the room just the way he wanted it, but he was excited to make it happen. He planned to involve the preschoolers in the final stages, selecting and arranging equipment and materials in the learning centers. He felt it was important to include the children in setting up the classroom. It was their space, and he felt they should have some say in their classroom design.

## Evaluating the learning environment

Even with careful planning, there is no guarantee that your learning environment will work as smoothly as you'd hoped. Observe and assess how children, teachers, and other staff interact within the environment. Early childhood environments need to be carefully evaluated and assessed on an annual basis. Evaluate the entire setting, including the playground, hallways, and bathrooms.

As you make changes, observe their effects and decide whether you have achieved your goals. Make further changes based on your observations. Begin the cycle again by considering whether your educational philosophy and goals are in alignment with your current situation. Be particularly attentive to ways in which the environment supports new program objectives. For example, if the program just added a technology objective, do you have enough computers and a well-equipped computer center?

Observing children as they play will tell you whether you have chosen the right equipment, materials, and toys. Remember that the effectiveness of equipment, materials, and toys depends on their placement, arrangement, accessibility, care, and maintenance.

Once you have completed your evaluation of your classroom environment, you should review, analyze, and communicate the results to your program's decision makers. The information gained from an evaluation is extremely valuable. You and your colleagues can use this information to implement your plan for an anti-bias curriculum within a high-quality, well-organized, and appropriately designed learning environment.

To support the physical, cognitive, and social development of children, the layout of the classroom can be aligned with YWCA Minneapolis standards as well as your state's licensing standards. Lesson planning and teaching in an anti-bias classroom will be distinctive, but it should follow the basic principles outlined in this chapter.

# Chapter Point Summary

1. Play-based learning is anti-bias teaching. Play is the vehicle that powers learning.
2. The true self of the child is also inextricably connected to the family.
3. Teachers should connect with students' families and include them in the classroom.
4. Play-based learning is supported through observation and assessments—in this way learning experiences are planned.
5. Anti-bias teachers follow the lead of children's interests by taking lesson side trips.
6. Lesson planning and teaching are done

    - with domain and standards in mind;
    - ahead of time by teachers; and
    - with children's input.

7. Lesson plans are able to change, and they should. Changes provide learning opportunities.
8. The environment should meet your state standards and include the curriculum's anti-bias principles.

We hope that after working with this book you have new thoughts and ideas for what your teaching can bring to the classroom. Each of us has had the opportunity to look at our own biases and evaluate how they affect our work in the field, and we encourage you to do the same. Working with an anti-bias approach means being open to evaluating your teaching, communication, and classroom on an ongoing basis. We believe that by being intentional with your approach, you can change the lives of the community you are working with. Come join us in our anti-bias journey!

# References

Abrams, Jasmine A., Faye Z. Belgrave, Chelsea D. Williams, and Morgan L. Maxwell. 2020. "African American Adolescent Girls' Beliefs About Skin Tone and Colorism." *Journal of Black Psychology* 46(2–3): 169–194. https://doi.org/10.1177/0095798420928194.

Ahmed, Sara. *Living a Feminist Life*. 2016. Durham, NC: Duke University Press.

Asher, Nina. 2003. "Engaging Difference: Towards a Pedagogy of Interbeing." *Teaching Education* 14, no. 3 (December): 235–247. https://doi.org/10.1080/1047621032000135159.

American Psychological Association. 2006. *APA Resolution on Prejudice, Stereotypes, and Discrimination.* www.apa.org/about/policy/prejudice.pdf.

———. 2012. *Dual Pathways to a Better America: Preventing Discrimination and Promoting Diversity.* www.apa.org/pubs/info/reports/dual-pathways-report.pdf.

———. 2019. "Digital Guidelines: Promoting Healthy Technology Use for Children." December 12. www.apa.org/helpcenter/digital-guidelines.

Becker, Brandon D., Kathleen C. Gallagher, and Robert C. Whitaker. 2017. "Teachers' Dispositional Mindfulness and the Quality of Their Relationships with Children in Head Start Classrooms." *Journal of School Psychology* 65 (December): 40–53. https://doi.org/10.1016/j.jsp.2017.06.004.

Beneke, Margaret R., Caryn C. Park, and Jordan Taitingfong. 2019. "An Inclusive, Anti-Bias Framework for Teaching and Learning about Race with Young Children." *Young Exceptional Children* 22, no. 2 (November): 74–86. https://doi.org/10.1177/1096250618811842.

Bennett, Susan V., AnnMarie Alberton Gunn, Guda Gayle-Evans, Estanislado S. Barrera IV, and Cynthia B. Leung. 2018. "Culturally Responsive Literacy Practices in an Early Childhood Community." *Early Childhood Education Journal* 46, no. 2 (March): 241–248.

Bian, Lin, Sarah-Jane Leslie, and Andrei Cimpian. 2018. "Evidence of Bias against Girls and Women in Contexts That Emphasize Intellectual Ability." *American Psychologist* 73(9): 1139–1153. https://doi.org/10.1037/amp0000427.

Biddle, Julie K. 2012. *The Three Rs of Leadership: Building Effective Early Childhood Programs through Relationships, Reciprocal Learning, and Reflection.* Ypsilanti, MI: HighScope Press.

Bronfenbrenner, Urie, and Stephen J. Ceci. 1994. "Nature-Nuture Reconceptualized in Developmental Perspective: A Bioecological Model." *Psychological Review* 101(4): 568–586.

Butler, Gary, Nastasja De Graaf, Bernadette Wren, and Polly Carmichael. 2018. "Assessment and Support of Children and Adolescents with Gender Dysphoria." *Archives of Disease in Childhood* 103(7): 631–36. https://doi.org/10.1136/archdischild-2018-314992.

Cheatham, Gregory A., and Sylvia Nyegenye. 2017. "Linguistic Differences with Bilingual Parents Who Are Immigrants: Words for Dialoguing about Young Children." *Early Childhood Education Journal* 45, no. 5 (July): 685–692. https://doi.org/10.1007/s10643-016-0803-0.

Cholewa, Blaire and West-Olatunji, Cirecie. 2008. "Exploring the Relationship Among Cultural Discontinuity, Psychological Distress, and Academic Outcomes with Low-Income, Culturally Diverse Students." *Professional School Counseling,* 12(1). https://doi.org/10.1177/2156759x0801200106.

Civitillo, Sauro, Linda P. Juang, and Maja K. Schachner. 2018. "Challenging Beliefs about Cultural Diversity in Education: A Synthesis and Critical Review of Trainings with Pre-Service Teachers." *Educational Research Review* 24, 67–83. https://doi.org/10.1016/j.edurev.2018.01.003.

Curbow, Barbara, Kai Spratt, Antoinette Ungaretti, Karen McDonnell, and Steven Breckler. 2000. "Development of the Child Care Worker Job Stress Inventory." *Early Childhood Research Quarterly* 15(4): 515–536.

Danniels, Erica, and Angela Pyle. 2018. "Defining Play-Based Learning." *Encyclopedia on Early Childhood Development.* www.child-encyclopedia.com/play-based-learning /according-experts/defining-play-based-learning.

Davidson, Christina, and Chris Edwards-Groves. 2020. "Producing and Closing Down Multiple-Response Sequences During Whole-Class Talk in an Early Years Classroom." *Language and Education* 34(3): 1–19.

Denham, Susanne A., Hideko H. Bassett, and Susanne L. Miller. 2017. "Early Childhood Teachers' Socialization of Emotion: Contextual and Individual Contributors." *Child & Youth Care Forum* 46(6): 805–24.

Derman-Sparks, Louise, and Julie Olsen Edwards. 2010. *Anti-Bias Education for Young Children and Ourselves.* Washington, DC: National Association for the Education of Young Children.

Derman-Sparks, Louise, Debbie LeeKeenan, and John Nimmo. 2015. *Leading Anti-Bias Early Childhood Programs: A Guide for Change.* New York: Teachers College Press.

DiAngelo, Robin J. 2018. *White Fragility: Why It's so Hard for White People to Talk about Racism.* Boston: Beacon.

Doucet, Fabienne. 2017. "What Does a Culturally Sustaining Learning Climate Look Like?" *Journal of Theory into Practice* 56(3): 195–204. https://doi.org/10.1080/00405841.2017.1354618.

Douglass, Anne, and Jody Hoffer Gittell. 2012. "Transforming Professionalism: Relational Bureaucracy and Parent–Teacher Partnerships in Child Care Settings." *Journal of Early Childhood Research* 10(3): 267–281. https://doi.org/10.1177/1476718X12442067.

Essary, Jessica, and Tunde Szecsi. 2018. "Friendships Overcome Ignorance and Misconceptions: Teacher Candidates' Exposure to a Foreign Culture in an Online Cross-National E-Pals Project." *Journal of Ethnic and Cultural Studies* 5(1): 41–57.

Endo, Hidehiro, Paul Chamness Reece-Miller, and Nicholas Santavicca. 2010. Surviving in the Trenches: A Narrative Inquiry into Queer Teachers' Experiences and Identity. *Teaching and Teacher Education*, 26(4): 1023–1030.

Fenech, Marianne, Jennifer Sumsion, and Wendy Shepherd. 2010. "Promoting Early Childhood Teacher Professionalism in the Australian Context: The Place of Resistance." *Contemporary Issues in Early Childhood* 11(1): 89–105. https://doi.org/10.2304/ciec.2010.11.1.89.

Fenton, Patrice, Lydia Ocasio-Stoutenburg, and Beth Harry. 2017. "The Power of Parent Engagement: Sociocultural Considerations in the Quest for Equity." *Journal of Theory into Practice* 56(3): 214–225. https://doi.org/10.1080/00405841.2017.1355686.

Gay, Geneva, and Kipchoge Kirkland. 2003. "Developing Cultural Critical Consciousness and Self-Reflection in Preservice Teacher Education." *Journal of Theory into Practice* 42(3): 181–187.

Gibbons, Andrew N. 2011. "The Incoherence of Curriculum: Questions Concerning Early Childhood Teacher Educators." *Australasian Journal of Early Childhood* 36(1): 9–15.

Gilliam, Walter S., Angela N. Maupin, Chin R. Reyes, Maria Accavitti, and Frederick Shic. 2016. *Do Early Educators' Implicit Biases Regarding Sex and Race Relate to Behavior Expectations and Recommendations of Preschool Expulsions and Suspensions?* Yale University Child Study Center. New Haven, CT.

Goldberg, Abbie E., Kaitlin Black, Kristin Sweeney, and April Moyer. 2017. "Lesbian, Gay, and Heterosexual Adoptive Parents' Perceptions of Inclusivity and Receptiveness in Early Childhood Education Settings." *Journal of Research in Childhood Education* 31(1): 141–159.

Gonzalez-Mena, Janet. 2008. *Diversity in Early Care and Education: Honoring Differences,* 5th ed. New York: McGraw-Hill Humanities/Social Sciences/Languages.

Gopnik, Alison. 2012. "Scientific Thinking in Young Children: Theoretical Advances, Empirical Research, and Policy Implications." *Science* 337(6102): 1623–27. https://doi.org/10.1126 /science.1223416.

Han, Suejung. 2017. "Attachment Insecurity and Openness to Diversity: The Roles of Self-Esteem and Trust." *Journal of Personality and Individual Differences* 111 (June): 291–296. https://doi .org/10.1016/j.paid.2017.02.033.

Heinecken, Dawn. 2020. "The Heart of the Game: Girls, Sports and the Limits of 'Empowerment.'" *Journal of Sport and Social Issues,* 0193723519898705.

hooks, bell. 2014. *Teaching to Transgress: Education as the Practice of Freedom.* New York: Routledge.

Jardine, David W. 2017. *Back to the Basics of Teaching and Learning: Thinking the World Together.* Oxfordshire, UK: Routledge.

Kagan, Sharon Lynn, Kristie Kauerz, and Kate Tarrant. 2008. *The Early Care and Education Teaching Workforce at the Fulcrum: An Agenda for Reform.* New York: Teachers College Press.

Kendi, Ibram X. 2019. *How to Be an Antiracist.* New York: One World/Ballantine.

Knopf, Herman T., and Kevin J. Swick. 2007. "How Parents Feel about Their Child's Teacher/ School: Implications for Early Childhood Professionals." *Early Childhood Education Journal* 34(4): 291–296.

———. 2008. "Using Our Understanding of Families to Strengthen Family Involvement." *Early Childhood Education Journal* 35(5): 419–427. https://doi.org/10.1007/s10643-007-0198-z.

Krasnoff, Basha. 2016. *Culturally Responsive Teaching: A Guide to Evidence-Based Practices for Teaching All Students Equitably.* Portland, Oregon: Region X Equity Assistance Center Education Northwest.

Levine, Robert V. 2015. "Time and Culture." In *Noba Textbook Series: Psychology,* edited by Robert Biswas-Diener and Edward Diener. Champaign, IL: DEF Publishers. https://nobaproject. com/modules/time-and-culture.

Lin, Miranda, Vickie E. Lake, and Diana Rice. 2008. "Teaching Anti-Bias Curriculum in Teacher Education Programs: What and How." *Teacher Education Quarterly* 35, no. 2 (Spring): 187–200.

McFarland-Piazza, Laura, and Rachel Saunders. 2012. "Hands-On Parent Support in Positive Guidance: Early Childhood Professionals as Mentors." *Australasian Journal of Early Childhood* 37(1): 65–73. https://doi.org/10.1177/183693911203700108.

Matute, Alexandra Arraiz, Luna Da Silva, Karleen Pendleton Jiménez, and Amy Smith. 2020. "The Sex of It All: Outness and Queer Women's Digital Storytelling in Teacher Education." *Teaching Education,* 31(1): 98-111.

Meece, Darrell, and Kimberly O'Kelley Wingate. 2009. "Providing Early Childhood Teachers with Opportunities to Understand Diversity and the Achievement Gap." *Journal of the Southeastern Regional Association of Teacher Educators* 19, no. 1 (Winter): 36–42.

Minnesota Department of Education. 2020. "Early Childhood Indicators of Progress." https://education.mn.gov/MDE/dse/early/highqualel/ind.

NAEYC (National Association for the Education of Young Children) and NAECS/SDE (National Association of Early Childhood Specialists in State Departments of Education). 2003. "Early Childhood Curriculum, Assessment, and Program Evaluation: Building an Effective, Accountable System in Programs for Children Birth through Age 8." Joint position statement. www.naeyc.org/sites/default/files/globally-shared/downloads/PDFs/resources/position-statements/pscape.pdf.

———. 2002. "Early Learning Standards: Creating the Conditions for Success." www.naeyc.org/sites/default/files/globally-shared/downloads/PDFs/resources/position-statements/position_statement.pdf.

NAEYC (National Association for the Education of Young Children). 2019. *Advancing Equity in Early Childhood Education: A Position Statement.* NAEYC. www.naeyc.org/resources/position-statements/equity.

Nimmo, John, Mona M. Abo-Zena, and Debbie LeeKeenan. 2019. "Finding a Place for the Religious and Spiritual Lives of Young Children and Their Families: An Anti-Bias Approach." *Young Children* 74, no. 5 (November): 37–45. www.antibiasleadersece.com/wp-content/uploads/2019/12/Nimmo-religion-YC-2019.pdf.

Northouse, Peter Guy. 2018. *Leadership: Theory and Practice.* 8th ed. Thousand Oaks, CA: Sage Publications.

Park, Caryn C. 2011. "Young Children Making Sense of Racial and Ethnic Differences: A Sociocultural Approach." *American Educational Research Journal* 48, no. 2 (April): 387–420. https://doi.org/10.3102/0002831210382889.

Priest, Jacob B, Shardé McNeil Smith, Sarah B. Woods, and Patricia N. E. Roberson. 2020. "Discrimination, Family Emotional Climate, and African American Health: An Application of the BBFM." *Journal of Family Psychology* 34(5): 598–609.

Quinan, C.L. 2016. "Kinsey Scale." The Wiley Blackwell Encyclopedia of Gender and Sexuality Studies (eds. A. Wong, M. Wickramasinghe, r. hoogland, and N. A. Naples). https://doi.org/10.1002/9781118663219.wbegss555.

Riley, Kathleen, and Kathryn Solic. 2017. "'Change Happens beyond the Comfort Zone': Bringing Undergraduate Teacher-Candidates into Activist Teacher Communities." *Journal of Teacher Education* 68(2): 179–192. https://doi.org/10.1177/0022487116687738.

Rodd, Jillian. 2012. *Leadership in Early Childhood.* Maidenhead, Birkshire, UK: McGraw-Hill Education.

Sullivan, Debra Ren-Etta. 2016. *Cultivating the Genius of Black Children: Strategies to Close the Achievement Gap in the Early Years.* St. Paul, MN: Redleaf Press.

Sumsion, Jennifer. 2000. "Negotiating Otherness: A Male Early Childhood Educator's Gender Positioning." *International Journal of Early Years Education*, 8(2): 129–140. https://doi.org/10.1080/09669760050046174.

Taggart, Amanda. 2017. "The Role of Cultural Discontinuity in the Academic Outcomes of Latina/o High School Students." *Education and Urban Society*, 49(8): 731–761.

Taylor, Meaghan Elizabeth, and Wanda Boyer. 2020. "Play-Based Learning: Evidence-Based Research to Improve Children's Learning Experiences in the Kindergarten Classroom." *Early Childhood Education Journal* 48(2): 127–133.

Tehee, Melissa, Devon Isaacs, and Melanie M. Domenech Rodríguez. 2020. "The Elusive Construct of Cultural Competence." In *Handbook of Cultural Factors in Behavioral Health*, edited by Lorraine T. Benuto, Frances R. Gonzalez, and Jonathan Singer, 11–24. Cham, Switzerland: Springer.

Telford, Rohan M., Richard D. Telford, Lisa S. Olive, Thomas Cochrane, and Rachel Davey. 2016. "Why Are Girls Less Physically Active Than Boys? Findings from the LOOK Longitudinal Study." *PloS One* 11(3): 1–11. https://doi.org/10.1371/journal.pone.0150041.

Thibodeaux, Tilisa, Drake Curette, Stacey Bumstead, Andrea Karlin, and Gayle Butaud. 2020. "Gauging Pre-Service Teachers' Awareness of Dialectical Code Switching in Classroom Settings." *Journal of Education*, 200(2): 120–129. https://doi.org/10.1177/0022057419877399.

Tokić, Ružica. 2018. "Motivation of Male Students for Preschool Teacher Profession." *Open Journal for Educational Research* 2(1): 31–44. https://doi.org/10.32591/coas.ojer.0201.03031t.

Ullucci, Kerri, and Dan Battey. 2011. "Exposing Color Blindness/Grounding Color Consciousness: Challenges for Teacher Education." *Urban Education* 46(6): 1195–1225. https://doi.org/10.1177/0042085911413150.

Van Laere, Katrien, Michel Vandenbroeck, Griet Roets, and Jan Peeters. 2014. "Challenging The Feminisation of the Workforce: Rethinking the Mind–Body Dualism in Early Childhood Education and Care." *Gender and Education* 26, no. 3 (May): 232–245. https://doi.org/10.1080/09540253.2014.901721.

Weisner, Thomas S. 2008. "The Urie Bronfenbrenner Top 19: Looking Back at His Bioecological Perspective." *Mind, Culture, and Activity* 15(3): 258–262.

Whitebook, Marcy, Caitlin McLean, Lea J. E. Austin, and Bethany Edwards. 2018. *Early Childhood Workforce Index 2018*. Berkeley: Center for the Study of Child Care Employment, University of California.

Whorrall, Jennifer, and Sonia Q. Cabell. 2016. "Supporting Children's Oral Language Development in the Preschool Classroom." *Early Childhood Education Journal* 44(4): 335–341.

Williams, K. E. 2018. "Moving to the beat: Using music, rhythm, and movement to enhance self-regulation in early childhood classrooms." *International Journal of Early Childhood*, 50(1): 85–100.

Williams, K. E., and D. Berthelsen. 2019. "Implementation of a rhythm and movement intervention to support self-regulation skills of preschool-aged children in disadvantaged communities." *Psychology of Music*, 47(6): 800–820.

Yogman, Michael, Andrew Garner, Jeffrey Hutchinson, Kathy Hirsh-Pasek, Roberta Michnick Golinkoff, Committee on Psychosocial Aspects of Child and Family Health, and Council on Communications and Media. 2018. "The Power of Play: A Pediatric Role in Enhancing Development in Young Children." *Pediatrics* 142, no. 3 (September): e20182058. https://doi.org/10.1542/peds.2018-2058.

Zeichner, Ken, and Katrina Yan Liu. 2010. "A Critical Analysis of Reflection as a Goal for Teacher Education." In *Handbook of Reflection and Reflective Inquiry*, edited by Nona Lyons, 67–84. Boston: Springer.

# Index

abilities, self-reflective practice exercise for unique, 44

Abo-Zena, Mona, 23

Abrams, Jasmine, 22

activism goals, 29, 66

Advancing Equity in Early Childhood Education (NAEYC), 46

African Americans, racism in lives of, 9

Ahmed, Sara, 23

American Psychological Association (APA)
on bias, 9
digital guidelines, 93
on diversity, 71
on "self-revealing interaction," 117

analytical thinking, 101–103

anti-bias education
goals, 27–29, 66
summary, 30

*Anti-Bias Education for Young Children and Ourselves* (Derman-Sparks and Olsen Edwards), 9, 27–29

anti-bias learning experiences
for changes over time, 75
for community, people, and relationships, 73
for computer knowledge, 94
for discovering, acting, and applying strategies in science, 110
for dramatic play, 100
for emergent reading skills, 91
for emergent writing skills, 93
for emotional security, 68
for exploring and expression, 97
for fine-motor skills, 114
for geometry, spatial thinking, and data analysis, 105–107
for healthy and safe living practices, 116
information processing and utilization, 84
interest and persistence, 83
for inventiveness, problem solving, and curiosity, 81
for large-motor skills, 111–113

for listening, understanding, communicating, and speaking, 88
for measurement, 104
for music and movement, 98
for numerals and patterns, 103
nurturing identity and self-esteem of each student as goals of, 46
for self-awareness, 70
for social understandings and relationships, 77
using mathematical concepts, 101

Approaches to Learning domain (AL)
as foundational to future learning skills in older children, 78
mistakes as learning opportunities, 78
standards, 78
1. inventiveness, problem solving, and curiosity, 79–81
2. interest and persistence, 81–83
3. information processing and utilization, 83–85

arts
communication through, 95
fine-motor skills and, 113–114
fostering during play, 95–96
mathematics and, 105
*See also* Creativity and Arts domain (CA)

Asher, Nina, 9

assessments. *See* observation and assessment; YWCA observation and assessment system

Bassett, Hideko, 120

Becker, Brandon, 128

behaviors
practicing healthy and safe, 115–116
requiring teacher attention, 65
teachers' expectations of children, 108
teachers modeling, 150

Beneke, Margaret R., 11

Bennett, Susan, 13

Bian, Lin, 108

bias
    described, 9, 13
    discrimination and, 9, 14
    examining own, 41–42
    lack of routine, systematized observation
      and assessment and, 121
    *See also* anti-bias education; gender bias;
      racism
body language, 58
books and "tourism" route of diversity, 89
Boyer, Wanda, 99
Bronfenbrenner, Urie, 12–13, 32
Butler, Gary, 18

Cabell, Sonia, 144, 149
Ceci, Stephen, 12–13
celebration, as part of YMCA observation and
    assessment system, 130–131
Cheatham, Gregory, 56–57
child development, human ecology model,
    12–13
children with disabilities
    adapting environment for, 151–152, 154
    planning for needs of, 27
    spectrum of, 6
Cimpian, Andrei, 108
civil rights, YWCA and, 2–4
code switching, 86–87
cognitive diversity
    accommodating for, 27
    self-study questions, 28
colloquialisms, 86–87
communication
    addressing styles of, 40–41
    comments indicating bias, 70–71
    cultural systems and, 23–24, 86–87
    eye contact and, 38–39
    information sharing between families and
      teachers
      daily, 58
      ensuring successful, 58–59
      first meetings, 57
      fostering open, 50–52
      observations and assessments and,
        120–122, 129
      planned, 58

nonverbal, 38–39, 58
personal space and, 38
racism and, 86–87
responsiveness to family and, 32
self-reflective practice exercise for, 38–40
smiling and, 38
speaking and listening, 39
through arts, 95
time concepts in, 39–40
*See also* Language and Literacy domain (LL)
computer knowledge, 93–94
concepts of time, 39–40
consistency, 151
Creativity and Arts domain (CA)
    communication and, 95
    standards, 95
      1. exploring and expression, 95–97
      2. music and movement, 97–98
      3. dramatic play, 98–100
critical awareness, described, 31
*Cultivating the Genius of Black Children*
    (Sullivan), 20
cultural bias
    racism and, 20–22
    self-reflective practice to uncover, 33
    self-study questions about, 26
    stepping out of own cultural expectations
      and, 47–48
    steps to avoid, 24
cultural systems
    acknowledging and respecting, 55–56
    books taking "tourism" route of, 89
    communication and, 23–24, 86–87
    ECE centers and, 13
    families and early childhood teachers as part
      of, 32
    fine-motor skills and, 113–114
    individual's personal, as nested in larger, 23
Curbow, Barbara, 40
curiosity, 79–81, 99

dancing, 97–98
Danniels, Erica, 151
Da Silva, Luna, 18–19
data analysis, 105–107
Davidson, Christina, 39

Denham, Susanne, 120

Derman-Sparks, Louise
    goals of anti-bias early childhood education, 27–29, 66
    importance of self-reflective practice, 31
    resource on bias, 9

developmental goals, meeting, through play, 7

dialogue, modeling and encouraging, 12

DiAngelo, Robin, 23

digital media knowledge, 93–94

direction, concepts of, 106

disabilities, children with
    adapting environment for, 151–152, 154
    planning for needs of, 27
    spectrum of, 6

discrimination
    defining, 14
    role of bias and prejudice in, 9

distance, concepts of, 106

diversity
    accommodating for physical, 27
    anti-bias goals, 28, 66
    books taking "tourism" route of, 89
    celebrating in lessons, 141–142
    children helping other children make sense of, 10–11, 12
    encouraging children to be comfortable with, 71
    preschool children's awareness of differences and, 10
    self-study questions about, 26, 28

Doucet, Fabienne, 44

*The Early Care and Education Teaching Workforce at the Fulcrum* (Kagan, Kauerz, and Tarrant), 16

early childhood education (ECE) programs
    cultural system and, 13
    "kindergarten readiness gap" and, 5
    public perception of value of, 16
    rating system for, 4
    teaching about race in, 9
    using observations and assessments to measure center-wide performance, 120

early childhood education (ECE) workforce, 16, 17–18
    *See also* teachers

early childhood leaders, characteristics, 8

*Early Childhood Workforce Index 2018* (Whitebook), 16

early learning standards
    activities for, 60
    making developmentally appropriate, 60
    play and, 71
    results of correctly implemented, 60

education, white Christian dominant narrative in, 23

Edwards-Groves, Chris, 39

emotional security, 66–68

emotions. *See* feelings and emotions; Social and Emotional Development domain (SE)

Endo, Hidehiro, 19

environments
    adapting for children with disabilities, 151–152, 154
    designing, 152, 157–158
    evaluating, 158
    layout, 153
    learning centers
    boundaries for, 153
    examples of, 155
    offering manageable number of choices for children, 157
    safety, 152–153, 157
    tools, equipment, and materials, 155–157
    traffic flow, 154

equality versus equity, 81

Essary, Jessica, 32

eye contact and communication, 38–39

fact words, example of using, 11

family/families
    as center of students' development, 141–142
    communication and responsiveness to, 32
    defining, 46
    as foundation as child's understanding of world, 32
    helping plan learning, 148
    importance of partnership with, 46–47

multiple ways of being and recognizing, 47–48
as part of cultural system, 32
as primary resource for understanding child, 27
relationship goals with
    acknowledging and respecting culture, 55–56
    creating support networks for, 53–55
    information sharing, 56–59
    recognizing and respecting each other; sharing power and decision-making with, 49–53
    summary, 59
self-study questions about, 28
*See also* information sharing between families and teachers *under* communication; parents

feelings and emotions
    child's skills in managing, as foundation for all other learning, 129
    expressing through music, 97
    understanding, 77
    *See also* Social and Emotional Development domain (SE)

fine-motor skills, 113–114

flexibility
    importance of, 147–148
    practices to foster, 149–151
    YWCA Minneapolis anti-bias curriculum and, 6

flight, fright, or freeze response, 65

Gallagher, Kathleen, 128

gay people, as ECE teachers, 18–19

gender
    books taking "tourism" route of, 89
    children disconnected from assigned, 18
    supporting nurturing for boys and girls, 17

gender bias
    comments indicating, 70
    ECE workforce and, 16, 17–18
    fighting, 17
    gender-nonconforming clothes and, 18
    motor skills and, 112
    in science, 108

gendered colorism, 22

gender expression
    fluidity of, 19
    by gay people, 18–19
    gender-nonconforming clothes and, 18

geometry, 105–107

gestures, 85–86, 87

Gibbons, Andrew, 23

Gilliam, Walter, 108

Givens, Phebe Mae, 2, *2*

Goldberg, Abbie, 47

Gopnik, Alison, 107–108, 134

Han, Suejung, 50

hand-eye coordination, 113–114

health and stressors, 9

Height, Dorothy, 3

Heinecken, Dawn, 112

hooks, bell, 22

*How to Be an Antiracist* (Kendi), 13

human ecology model, 12–13, 32

humor, 150

I am from self-reflective exercises, 35–38

icebreaker activities, self-reflective practice exercise for unique abilities, 44

identity goals
    artistic expression and, 95
    elements of, 28, 66
    nurturing each student's, 46

information, processing and using, 83–85

interruptions, tolerance for, 81

inventive thinking, 79–81

Isaacs, Devon, 31

Jiménez, Karleen Pendleton, 18–19

justice goals
    elements of, 28, 66
    guiding students to internal sense of, 78

Kagan, Sharon Lynn, 16

Kauerz, Kristie, 16

Kendi, Ibram X., 13, 22

Knopf, Herman, 32, 52

Language and Literacy domain (LL)
  standards, 85
    1. listening, communicating, and speaking, 85–88
    2. emergent reading skills, 89–91
    3. emergent writing skills, 91–93
    4. computer knowledge, 93–94
large-motor skills, 111–113
*Leadership in Early Childhood* (Rodd), 8
learning domains
  alignment to YWCA Minneapolis curriculum, 62
  Approaches to Learning. *See* Approaches to Learning domain (AL)
  Creativity and the Arts. *See* Creativity and the Arts domain (CA)
  Language and Literacy (LL). *See* Language and Literacy domain (LL)
  Mathematical Development. *See* Mathematical Development domain (MD)
  overview of, 61
  Physical and Motor Development. *See* Physical and Motor Development domain (PM)
  Scientific Thinking. *See* Scientific Thinking domain (ST)
  Social and Emotional Development. *See* Social and Emotional Development domain (SE)
  standards alignment and, 62–63
  summary, 117
  using balanced perspective, 117
  YMCA lesson plan themes and, 139–141
LeeKeenan, Debbie, 23, 31
Leslie, Sarah-Jane, 108
Levine, Robert, 39
limits, testing, 65
listening, 142, 149
Liu, Katrina Yan, 31
*Living a Feminist Life* (Ahmed), 23
location, concepts of, 106

marginalized groups
  importance of recognizing and nurturing individuality of, 47
  undoing unfairness to, 13–15
Mathematical Development domain (MD)
  arts and, 105
  elements included in, 100
  standards, 101
    1. numerals and patterns, 101–103
    2. measurement, 103–104
    3. geometry, spatial thinking, and data analysis, 105–107
Matute, Alexandra Arraiz, 18–19
McFarland-Piazza, Laura, 32
measurement, 103–104
Melissa Tehee, 31
memories, self-reflective exercise, 34–35
men, in ECE workforce and, 17–18
microaggressions
  defining, 14
  occurrence of, 13
Miller, Mrs. W. A., 2, *2*
Miller, Susanne, 120
mindfulness, 129
mind maps, 43
mistakes, as learning opportunities, 78
motor skills
  fine, 113–114
  large, 111–113
music, 97–98

name-recognition and writing, 91
National Association for the Education of Young Children (NAEYC)
  Advancing Equity in Early Childhood Education, 46
  assessment and program evaluation, 117
  early learning standards, 60
  Power to the Profession movement, 16
  teachers as guiding development of children, 135
National Association of Early Childhood Specialists in State Departments of Education (NAECS/SDE), 60, 117
needs versus wants, 81

networks of support, 53–55

Nimmo, John, 23, 31

nonverbal communication, 38–39, 58

nurturing, supporting for boys and girls, 17

Nyegenye, Sylvia, 56–57


observation and assessment
    authentic, ongoing, and structured, 120–122
    benefits of routine, systematized, 121
    common systems for, 119
    documentation example, 139–140
    of learning environment, 158
    during play, 121–122
    reasons for, 117–119
    summary, 132
    unpacking bias and, 117
    *See also* YMCA observation and assessment
      system

Olsen Edwards, Julie
    goals of anti-bias early childhood education,
      27–29, 66
    resource on bias, 9


Parent Aware, 5

parents
    as children's primary educators and experts
      about, 49
    communication with
    fostering open, with teachers, 50–52
    observations and assessments and, 120–122,
      129
    defining, 46
    *See also* family/families

Park, Caryn C.
    on children helping other children make
      sense of racial and ethnic differences,
      10–11, 12
    on teachers' reactions to sensitive topics, 11

patterning, 101–103

people with gender-nonconforming identities,
    gender expression by, 18–19

persistence, 81–83

"personal best" culture, 74

personal bias, examining, 41–42

Physical and Motor Development domain
    (PM)
    arts and, 113–114
    positive identity and, 111
    standards, 111
      1. large-motor skills, 111–113
      2. fine-motor skills, 113–114
      3. healthy and safe living practices,
        115–116

play
    arts and, 95–96
    dramatic, 83, 98–100
    early learning standards reached through, 71
    fostering high-quality, 134–135
    importance of, 134
    meeting developmental goals through, 7
    observation and assessment during,
      121–122
    with puzzles, 105
    self-directed, 121
    summary, 159
    time for, 81, 83
    as work of child, 99, 133
    writing opportunities in area for, 91
    YWCA lesson plan themes as jumping off
      point for, 136

Power to the Profession movement (NAEYC),
    16

prejudice
    bias as often preceding, 9
    defining, 14
    stereotypes leading to, 18

pretending, 83, 98–100

pretend reading, 89

Priest, Jacob, 9

problem-solving, 79–81, 85

proximity, concepts of, 106

puzzles, 105

Pyle, Angela, 151


race
    books taking "tourism" route of, 89
    teaching about, in early childhood
      education, 9

racism
    blaming victim, 20
    comments indicating, 70–71

communication and, 86–87

cultural bias and, 20–22

defining, 20

in lives of African Americans, 9

unlearning, 22

reading skills, 89–91

recitation, use of, 39

Reece-Miller, Paul Chamness, 19

regression, 65

"religious literacy," 23

responsive teaching, 142, 149

Rodd, Jillian, 8

Rodríguez, Melanie Domenech, 31

rules, differentiating between home and
school, 65

Santavicca, Nicholas, 19

Saunders, Rachel, 32

Scientific Thinking domain (ST)

discover, act, and apply strategies standard,
109–110

"doing science," 107

self-awareness, as Social and Emotional
Development standard, 68–70

self-esteem, nurturing each student's, 46

self-reflective practice
benefits of, 33, 117
critical awareness and, 31
described, 31
exercises for
1. earliest memories, 34–35
2. I am from (version 1), 35–36
2. I am from (version 2), 36–38
3. communication styles, 38–40
4. windows and doors, 41
5. examining personal bias, 41–42
6. triggers, 42–43
7. unique abilities, 44
importance of, 31–32
questions for, 33–34
social justice and, 31, 32
summary, 45
to uncover biases, 33
"self-revealing interaction," 117

self-soothing, 65

sexism. *See* gender bias

shapes, 105–107

Smith, Amy, 18–19

snow "recipe," 54–55

Social and Emotional Development domain
(SE)
anti-bias goals and, 66
behaviors requiring teacher attention, 65
as foundation for all other learning, 129
predictable daily routines, 64
standards, 64
1. emotional security, 66–68
2. self-awareness, 68–70
3. community, people, and relationships,
70–73
4. changes over time, 73–75
5. social understandings and
relationships, 75–77

social justice, self-reflective practice and, 31,
32

spatial thinking, 105–107

stereotypes
combating gender, 108
defining, 14
resulting in prejudice, 18
in sports, 112

stressors
bias as, 9
on teachers, 40–41, 120–121

stress response, 65

Sullivan, Debra Ren-Etta, 20, 47

Sumsion, Jennifer, 17

support networks, 53–55

Swick, Kevin, 32, 52

symbolic language, 85–86, 87

Szecsi, Tunde, 32

Taitingfong, Jordan, 11

Tarrant, Kate, 16

Taylor, Meaghan Elizabeth, 99

teachers
allowing children to explore their place in
world safely, 18
as asexual, 18–19

beliefs about children shape thinking and
    feeling of, 44
dominating conversations with children, 39
educational conversations with students,
    125–127
expectations of children's behaviors, 108
families and
    acknowledging and respecting culture of,
        55–56
    creating networks of support, 53–55
    fostering open communication, 50–52
    importance of partnership with, 46–47
    information sharing with, 56–59
    recognizing multiple forms of, 47–48
    sharing power and decision-making
        through recognition and respect for
        each other, 49–53
    summary of relationship goals, 59
gay individuals as, 18–19
as guiding development of children,
    135–137
as part of cultural system, 32
reactions to sensitive topics, 11–12
as role models, 150
self-perception, 18–19
sexism and, 16, 17–18
stressors on, 40–41, 120–121
tolerance for interruptions, 81
well-being of, 128–129
See also information sharing between
    families and teachers under
    communication

teaching strategies
    checklist for evaluation of, 141, 142
    documenting learning experiences, 139–140
    following children's leads, 137–139, 142–
        146, 149
    phrases to help capture children's ideas, 144
    taking side trips, 146–147
Teaching to Transgress (hooks), 22
Telford, Rohan, 112
time concepts, 39–40
triggers, self-reflective practice exercise for
    examining, 42–43

unfairness, undoing, 13–15

Van Laere, Katrien, 16

wages, as example of market value, 16
wants versus needs, 81
Whitaker, Robert, 128
Whitebook, Marcy, 16
white Christian dominant narrative in
    education, 23
White Fragility: Why It's So Hard for White
    People to Talk about Racism (DiAngelo), 23
whole child, 12–13
Whorrall, Jennifer, 144, 149
"why" questions, 79
windows and doors self-reflective practice
    exercise, 41
women
    building respect for, 17
    YWCA and, 2–4, 3
    See also gender; specific individuals

Yogman, Michael, 133
YWCA
    basic information about, 1
    civil rights and, 2–4
    Early Childhood Education Department,
        3, 4
    Minneapolis building, 2, 2
    women and, 2–4, 3
YWCA Minneapolis anti-bias curriculum
    accreditation of, 5
    alignment to learning domains, 62
    flexibility and, 6
    lesson plans
        themes, 136
        using impromptu experiences, 137–139
    objectives, 6
    principles of, 5
    requirements of, 4–5
    steps in preparing, 5
    summary, 159
YWCA observation and assessment system
    celebration and, 130–131
    diagram of, 130
    example of process, 125–127
    principles guiding, 119, 133
    purposes of, 119
    sample observation and documentation
        tool, 124

schedule for, 122–124
steps in process, 127–128
using, 129–132

Zeichner, Ken, 31